On the cover: Monogram designed by Bruce Rogers for Carl H. Pforzheimer.

Opposite: Shelley's sketches on the front pastedown endpaper of the vellum notebook containing his draft of *A Philosophical View of Reform* (1819–?1820) and other fragments.

The Carl H. Pforzheimer Collection of

Shelley and

A History,

a Biography,

and

a Guide

His Circle

Stephen Wagner

Doucet Devin Fischer

The New York Public Library, 1996

**Opposite: The Pforzheimer
Reading Room, restored in 1993
by Peter Marino and Associates,
is furnished with antiques from the
original collector's library.
Photograph © Peter Aaron/ESTO.
All rights reserved.**

Library of Congress Cataloging-in-Publication Data

Wagner, Stephen, 1941-
      The Carl H. Pforzheimer Collection of Shelley and His Circle :
a history, a biography, and a guide / Stephen Wagner, Doucet Devin
Fischer.
         p.   cm.
      ISBN 0-87104-443-9 (pbk. : alk. paper)
      ISBN 0-87104-444-7 (hc : alk. paper)
      1. Shelley, Percy Bysshe, 1792-1822–Library resources–New York
(State)–New York. 2. Shelley, Percy Bysshe, 1792-1822–Friends and
associates–Library resources–New York (State)–New York. 3. English
poetry–Library resources–New York (State)–New York. 4. Carl H.
Pforzheimer Collection of Shelley and His Circle. 5. Poets,
English–19th century–Biography. I. Fischer, Doucet Devin. II. Carl H.
Pforzheimer Collection of Shelley and His Circle. III. New York
Public Library. IV. Title.
Z8815.W34   1996
[PR5433]
821'.7–dc20
                                                  96-22027
                                                    CIP

CONTENTS

ACKNOWLEDGMENTS

The authors are most grateful to the following
individuals:

For biographical details and background
information about the history of the Collection,
Mr. and Mrs. Carl H. Pforzheimer, Jr., Mihai H.
Handrea, and the late Kenneth Neill Cameron.

For encouragement, support, and guidance,
Rodney Phillips, Lisa Browar, Anne Skillion,
Karen Van Westering, and Marilan Lund.

For close reading and creative suggestions,
Donald H. Reiman and Daniel Dibbern.

And finally, special thanks for their astuteness and
expertise to our copy editor, Barbara Bergeron;
our designer, Doug Clouse; and our photographer,
Peter Bittner of Spring Street Digital, Inc.

STEPHEN WAGNER
Curator, Pforzheimer Collection

DOUCET DEVIN FISCHER
Co-Editor, Shelley and his Circle
The Carl and Lily Pforzheimer Foundation, Inc.

I

The Collection and the Collector

8   The Carl H. Pforzheimer Collection of Shelley and His Circle is one of the world's leading repositories for the study of English Romanticism. Its holdings consist of some 20,000 items, including books, manuscripts, letters, and other objects, chiefly from the late eighteenth and early nineteenth centuries. Dating back to the years after World War I – a time when many large private libraries were being dispersed – the Collection was the creation of Carl H. Pforzheimer, Sr. (1879–1957), who brought to the world of books and manuscripts the same qualities of shrewdness and determination that had already made him the country's most prominent dealer in oil securities.

Pforzheimer was born in New York City and was educated in its public schools. After leaving City College, sometime before 1898, the young Pforzheimer went to work as a runner on New York's curbside exchange for $4 a week. He did not remain in this subordinate position for long, however, and by the age of twenty-three had founded his own firm, which specialized in oil stocks at a time when Wall Street all but ignored the petroleum industry. As the century advanced so did his fortunes, paralleling America's growing infatuation with the automobile. In the ensuing years he would achieve preeminence, both as a financier and as a collector of rare books and manuscripts.

He is said to have begun his collection with a chance purchase from a bookstall on the banks of the Seine during a trip to Paris in 1906. By the 1920s collecting had turned into an obsession, and his purchases were ranging from incunables to modern fine-press editions, and included illuminated manuscripts, Bibles, children's books, as well as literary and historical works – both

Page 7: Carl H. Pforzheimer, Sr., 1879–1957.

English and American. This eclecticism was reflected in such acquisitions as a perfect copy of the Gutenberg Bible, an exquisitely illustrated Book of Hours, the suppressed first issue of *Alice's Adventures in Wonderland*, and important manuscripts by writers as varied as Dickens, Thoreau, and A. A. Milne. Despite these varied interests, however, he pursued certain projects with intensity and singlemindedness. His determination to seek out especially fine copies of the earlier "classics" of English literature, for example, resulted in a collection so distinguished and definitive that its catalogue, when it appeared in 1940, was immediately heralded as a standard bibliographical reference work. And today the famous three-volume *Carl H. Pforzheimer Library of English Literature 1475–1700*, designed by Bruce Rogers and Frederic Warde, and issued in a limited edition of 150 copies, has itself become a prized rare book.

At the same time that he was acquiring such bibliographic monuments as the Caxton edition of the *Recuyell of the Historyes of Troye* (the first book printed in the English language) and the four folios of Shakespeare, he adopted an original approach to works from a later period. When an extraordinary trove of Shelley material appeared on the market in 1920, it served as a catalyst for what would become a consuming passion: to build a collection that would document the private and creative lives of a small group of remarkably talented writers who flourished in England during the decades following the French Revolution. For along with the customary first editions and literary manuscripts, Pforzheimer bought up deeds, wills, tradesmen's bills, promissory notes, insurance policies, diaries, and above all correspondence – the letters which linked parents and children, husbands and wives, writers and publishers, friends, lovers, and enemies. In time, this aggregation of written matter would coalesce into what is now The Carl H. Pforzheimer Collection of Shelley and His Circle.

That a politically conservative entrepreneur like Pforzheimer would embrace a poet as radical as Shelley is

something of a paradox. The origins of his interest in the young poet remain unclear, but perhaps Shelley's social iconoclasm struck a responsive chord in a man known to have admired figures as diverse as Thomas Paine, H. L. Mencken, Ambrose Bierce, and Theodore Roosevelt – all because, as he put it, they "opposed the status quo." Certainly, next to his Gutenberg, he was proudest of the Shelley collection, and when he set out to catalogue it, he made another unconventional decision. He persuaded Kenneth Neill Cameron to give up a tenured position at Indiana University, luring him to New York with an offer to take charge of the project at double his professor's salary. The selection of an avowed Marxist must have raised a few eyebrows, but it was a logical choice. Cameron was not only the leading Shelley scholar of the time but also the author of a prizewinning biography. His *Shelley: Genesis of a Radical* had effectively destroyed the "ineffectual angel" image of the poet which had previously dominated twentieth-century literary discourse.

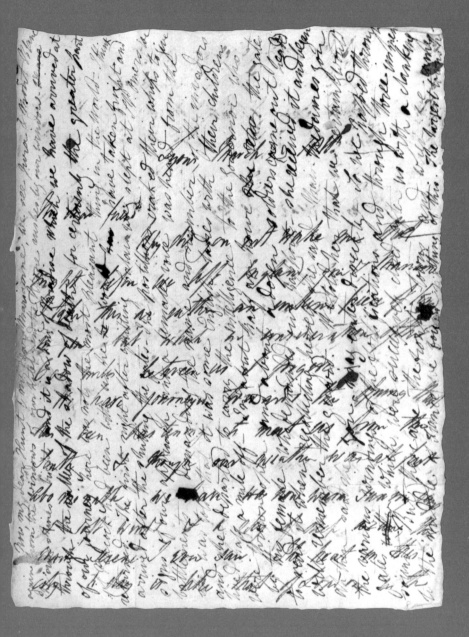

Opposite: Autograph double letter from Percy Bysshe and Mary
Wollstonecraft Shelley to Leigh and Marianne Hunt (March 22, 1818),
and detail (above). Crosswritten letters, common in the early nineteenth
century, were a means of circumventing the high postage rates of the
time. Mary Shelley's portion is written vertically.

Together, the scholar and the businessman soon came to realize that the unique nature of the materials demanded a departure from traditional methods. First they abandoned the alphabetical order characteristic of most catalogues in favor of a chronological arrangement; then they decided to expand the customary descriptive notes, providing instead a full transcription and commentary for each manuscript and augmenting them with biographical and contextual essays by leading scholars. Such a presentation, the two felt, would reveal the tangled roots of art and life and simultaneously create a sense of narrative continuity. Their vision was realized in the multi-volume publication *Shelley and his Circle, 1773–1822*, edited first by Cameron, then by Donald H. Reiman and Doucet Devin Fischer. This ongoing work – eight volumes have so far appeared – is a bibliographical hybrid: part catalogue, part collective biography, part social history, and part literary criticism. When the initial volumes appeared in 1961, they were widely recognized as having set new editorial standards for the presentation of nineteenth-century literary manuscripts. For the first time, the methods of textual analysis and description associated with Medieval and Renaissance texts were brought to bear on documents from the Romantic period.

Upon Pforzheimer's death in 1957, his collections became an asset of The Carl and Lily Pforzheimer Foundation, Inc. The library was transferred from his Park Avenue apartment to a suite of offices in midtown Manhattan, strategically chosen for its proximity to The New York Public Library, and for the next thirty years was administered as an independent research facility. Over time, some of the collections were sold – the Gutenberg Bible and the famous early English literature holdings went to the University of Texas – and some given away. The Shelley collection, however, continued to expand and the publication project grew along with it. Under the direction of Carl H. Pforzheimer, Jr., a number of spectacular manuscripts were added, among them the fair copy of Byron's *Beppo* and the

Esdaile Notebook, a small bound volume into which Shelley
had copied his earliest poetry.

Shortly before his death in March of 1994, Kenneth
Cameron reminisced about his early days working in Pforzheimer's Park Avenue apartment. In the study, as Cameron
recalled, Pforzheimer kept not one but three desks, all in a row:
one for business, one for his collections, and one for philan-
thropy. Cameron remembered him seated in an office chair –
one with wheels – propelling himself from desk to desk
as different matters came to mind. The story is emblematic,
for like other men of accomplishment from his generation,
Pforzheimer combined private success with public service,
donating his time to many educational, civic, and medical
institutions, including The New York Public Library, on whose
Board of Trustees he served for the last eight years of his life.

And it was, appropriately, The New York Public Library
that eventually became the home of his most treasured books
and manuscripts. It had always been Carl Pforzheimer's intention that in time his favorite offspring would become part of
a public institution. In 1986 this final wish was realized when
the Foundation presented The Carl H. Pforzheimer Collection
of Shelley and His Circle to The New York Public Library –
a gift underwritten by a generous endowment to allow for
future growth. Even in an institutional setting, however, the
spirit of the old Pforzheimer Library has been retained; a
recent renovation incorporates many of its original furnish-
ings and preserves much of its former ambience.

14

left to right:
William Godwin
Mary Wollstonecraft
Mary Shelley
Leigh Hunt
Lord Byron
(see List of Illustrations,
page 124, for full citations)

II

The Shelley Circle:
Dramatis Personæ

Shelley and the cast of characters – major and minor – that surrounded him represent an extraordinary confluence of literary talent, comparable perhaps to the Bloomsbury Group or the New England Transcendentalists. His friend and fellow poet, Lord Byron, wrote the most famous poetry of the time and his second wife, Mary Wollstonecraft Shelley, the most famous novel; her father, William Godwin, set forth the major work of political philosophy for the period and her mother, Mary Wollstonecraft, the defining work of feminism. Other close associates included Leigh Hunt, the poet, journalist, and editor; Thomas Love Peacock, the comic novelist and poet; and Edward John Trelawny, the writer and adventurer whose life itself was a work of invention. The Pforzheimer Collection contains extensive archives relating to all these writers as well as to many other literary figures less central to Shelley's life.

Percy Bysshe Shelley (1792–1822)

"Poets are the unacknowledged legislators of the World." There is an unintended irony to these final words of Shelley's *Defence of Poetry*: Shelley himself might well have become a legislator like his father, who served as a Member of Parliament. Heir to one of the wealthiest landowners in Sussex and Kent, the young Shelley was predestined for a career which had long ago been plotted: Eton, Oxford, the Grand Tour, and, at twenty-one, a seat in the House of Commons. Shelley, however, had an agenda of his own. While still a student, he managed to engineer a

NOTE: Passages marked with an asterisk (*) are taken from original documents now in the Pforzheimer Collection.

Page from Shelley's autograph note-book for *A Philosophical View of Reform* (1819–?1820), his longest and most ambitious prose work.

spectacular derailment – expulsion from the university followed quickly by an unsanctioned and socially unpalatable marriage that alienated him from his family. The unacknowledged legislator began his public career as an all-but-unacknowledged son.

And ended it as an all-but-unacknowledged poet. Few great writers have been less appreciated by their contemporaries. When Shelley drowned off the Italian coast in 1822, a few weeks before his thirtieth birthday, much of his writing was still unpublished. The first collection of his poems was brought out in 1824 by his young widow, Mary Shelley, author of *Frankenstein*. Subsequent editions would establish him as a literary cult figure and as a model for the next poetic generation, which included Browning and Tennyson. While such Victorian literati as the Pre-Raphaelites and Swinburne canonized Shelley for his lyric gifts and technical mastery, nineteenth-century radicals found other values in his writings: Owenites, Chartists, Fabian socialists, and Marxists alike responded to their political dimensions.

When Shelley was born, the French Revolution was progressing from its hopeful beginnings into that more sanguinary phase that has come to be known as the Reign of Terror. But it was the reactionary period following the Revolution that formed the ground of Shelley's poetic endeavor – the long, drawn-out wars, repression, and social injustice engendered by the realpolitik of men like Napoleon, Castlereagh, and Metternich. Perhaps no writer before him had so passionately and single-mindedly persisted in the effort to undermine an existing social order.

Early in his career, after several notable failures, Shelley turned away from quixotic political gestures, recognizing that any attempt to alter social and economic conditions without also changing the underlying structures of consciousness would be, in the end, self-defeating. His belief in the power of literature to effect such a transformation, and, hence, in the social mission of the Poet, stems from the hard-won conviction that the individual imagination remains the ultimate arbiter of reality.

The Pforzheimer Collection is the single most important repository of Shelley material in the western hemisphere and has amassed more of his letters than any other library in the world. Among its unique holdings are more than 300 items in the poet's hand, including an unmatched sequence of letters to his friend and rival poet, Lord Byron; correspondence with figures of literary consequence such as Leigh Hunt, Thomas Love Peacock, Horace Smith, E. J. Trelawny, William Godwin, and Mary Shelley; written exchanges with such friends and associates as T. J. Hogg, Claire Clairmont, John Gisborne, William Baxter, and Teresa Guiccioli; financial statements, checks, legal documents, and other records of his dealings with publishers and booksellers, carriage makers and upholsterers, landlords and hotel keepers. Literary manuscripts also form a prominent part of the Collection: the draft of the dedication to *The Cenci*; fair copies of "Athanase, a Fragment" and some later lyrics; sections of long poems such as *Prometheus Unbound*, *Laon and Cythna*, *Oedipus Tyrannus*, and *The Mask of Anarchy*; translations of Plato and Aristotle; and drafts of the essays "On Love" and "Speculations on Morals." In addition, the Collection possesses first and subsequent editions of his works, including several volumes, *Queen Mab* among them, heavily marked with his own revisions. It also has a substantial collection of books owned, read, and annotated by Shelley, including copies of Homer, Herodotus, Spinoza, and, most significantly, his intellectual vade mecum, Godwin's *Political Justice*. But the two real gems of the Collection are a pair of simple notebooks. In one, now known as the Esdaile Notebook, Shelley collected the texts of his earliest poems; in the other, he began his longest – though unfinished – prose work, *A Philosophical View of Reform*, a pragmatic essay on the political and social order. Together these two notebooks – one in marbled boards, the other bound in plain vellum – exemplify two polarities of Shelley's thought: the lyric and the proselytizing tendencies which alternated in both his life and works.

New Gods; like men, changing in ceaseless flow
live at hand as antient ones decay,
Heroes, & Kings & laws have plunged the world
in war

Sesostris, Caesar, & Ozyris come
Thou Moses! & Mahommed leave that glo
Destroyers! never shall your memory die
Approach pale Phantom to yon mouldering tom
Where all thy bones, hopes, curses & passions lie
And thou poor peasant when thou pass'st the grave
Where deep enthroned in monumental pride
Sleep low in dust the mighty & the brave
Where the mad conqueror whose gigantic stride
The Earth was too confined for, doth abide
Housing his bones amid a little clay
In gratitude to Natures Spirit bend

_____

+ To this innumerable host of legal murd
erers our own age affords numerous addenda
Federic of Prussia, Buonaparte, Suwarroff
Wellington & Nelson are the most skilful
& notorious scourges of that species of

and wait in still hope for thy better end

The Voyage

~~The Dreaming~~

A Fragment.

Devonshire — August 1812

Quenched is old Oceans rage.
Each boisterous wave that flung
it neck that writhed beneath the tempests
    Indignant up to Heaven
Now breathes in its sweet slumber
To mingle with the day
A spirit of tranquillity
Beneath the cloudless sun
The gently swelling main
Scatters a thousand colourings

the present day —

A bust of Shelley by Marianne Hunt and three oil paintings, likenesses of Shelley's father and mother by the noted portrait painter George Romney, and of Shelley's son William by the amateur painter and family friend Amelia Curran, also form part of the Collection. Other materials include an extensive archive of family papers: letters, legal documents, and memorabilia belonging to Shelley's grandfather, Sir Bysshe; his father, Sir Timothy; his son and daughter-in-law, Sir Percy Florence and Lady Jane; as well as other, more remote antecedents of the poet.

William Godwin (1756–1836)

Two generations of English poets and intellectuals fell under the spell of the political philosopher and social anarchist whose sun rose during the heady years following the fall of the Bastille. ("Throw aside your books of chemistry," Wordsworth reportedly said to a young admirer, "and read Godwin on Necessity!") The work he was referring to, *An Enquiry Concerning Political Justice* (1793), called for the transformation of political and social institutions through radical economic reform and argued that "perfectibility" – Godwin's term for human progress – was inevitable. He refined his arguments in a series of exchanges with Thomas Malthus (whose famous essay, *Of Population*, was conceived partly as a rejoinder to Godwin's melioristic philosophy) and particularized them in such novels as *Things as They Are; or, The Adventures of Caleb Williams* (1794), considered by some critics to be the first psychological thriller.

Though marriage was one of the conventions Godwin condemned in *Political Justice*, when Mary Wollstonecraft found herself expecting their child, the couple were quick enough to legitimize their own domestic arrangement, although they did continue to maintain separate households. Wollstonecraft died of childbed fever only five months later, just ten days after the birth of the infant Mary, future author of *Frankenstein* and wife of the

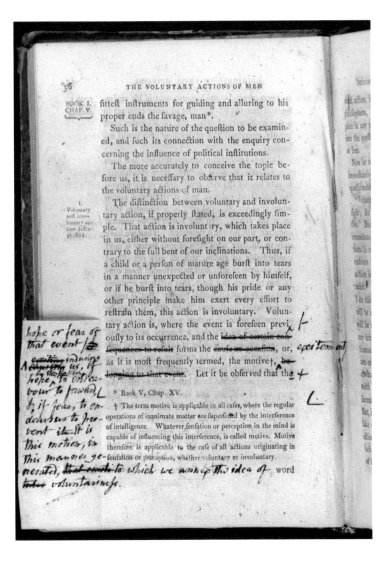

23

Pages 20–21: Pages from the Esdaile Notebook (1808–1813), in which Shelley copied his earliest poems. This collection was not published until 1964.

Above: Proof sheet for the third edition of Godwin's *Political Justice* (1798), with revisions in his hand.

poet Percy Bysshe Shelley. Four years later Godwin married again. With his second wife, the former Mary Jane Clairmont, he founded the Juvenile Library, an early publisher of children's literature. Both Godwins wrote stories for this enterprise, for the most part pseudonymously. However, their success, such as it was, depended on other contributions, among them the engravings of William Blake and the stories of Charles and Mary Lamb, whose *Tales from Shakespear* (first published in 1807) became a staple of the backlist. Perennially in debt, in his later years Godwin struggled to support his household with his pen, writing fiction, history, biography, textbooks, and topical essays. Although he continued to attract the occasional disciple, the man whom Shelley once called a "Mighty Eagle" was all but forgotten at the time of his death.

· IN THE COLLECTION ·

Among the major Godwin manuscripts in the Pforzheimer Collection are drafts of two novels, *Fleetwood* and *Cloudesley*, and of his last published work, *Lives of the Necromancers*, an odd compendium of superstitious lore. Another highlight is the proof copy of the 1798 edition of *Political Justice*, annotated with Godwin's own revisions and directions to the printer. Other items include a copy of the first edition of a third novel, *St. Leon*, with Godwin's revisions; an annotated copy of his book of essays, *The Enquirer*, along with a draft for one of its chapters, "Of Public and Private Education"; and a playbill for his drama *Antonio*, upon which Charles Lamb scribbled, "Damned with Universal Consent." In addition to first and subsequent editions of his works, the Collection embraces an extensive archive of Godwin's correspondence with leading political and literary figures of the day, among them Percy Bysshe Shelley, Mary Shelley, Edward Bulwer-Lytton, Dr. Charles Burney, Aaron Burr, S. T. Coleridge, J. P. Curran, Mary Hays, Elizabeth Inchbald, Edmund Kean, Thomas Malthus, John Howard Payne, Francis Place,

Thomas Clio Rickman, R. B. Sheridan, Madame de Staël, and Ludwig Tieck. In addition, a sizeable body of letters, book proposals, and publishing agreements document Godwin's relations with contemporary publishers like Charles Ollier, William Hone, William Blackwood, Edward Moxon, T. N. Longman, John Taylor (of Taylor & Hessey), Richard Bentley, Henry Colburn, Archibald Constable, and J. & G. Robinson. Other Godwin material in the Collection includes documents related to his ordination as a Dissenting minister, call slips for books read at the British Museum, a copy of his will, and a representative sample of the numerous promissory notes that so regularly punctuated his long life. Finally, the Pforzheimer Collection also includes copies of many of the children's books published by the Godwins' firm, the Juvenile Library.

Mary Wollstonecraft (1759–1797)

Mary Wollstonecraft's most important work, the impassioned *Vindication of the Rights of Woman* (1792), addressed the plight of the voiceless half of the human race passed over by architects of the revolutions in America and France. Like other advocates of social change, she placed her faith in reason and argued that education would break the mind-forged manacles that had kept women in submission through the ages. In polemic and fiction alike, education remained her central concern. Both *Thoughts on the Education of Daughters* (1787) and its companion piece, *Mary, a Fiction* (1788), argued for a revolution in the treatment of children; even in books written ostensibly for juveniles, like *Original Stories from Real Life* (1788), a similar subtext is present.

Wollstonecraft's opinions were formed by experience. She herself had survived a haphazard upbringing in a household headed by a harsh, despotic father and a neglectful mother. At eighteen she escaped, taking a position as companion

Mary Hays

A VINDICATION

OF THE

RIGHTS OF WOMAN:

WITH

STRICTURES

ON

POLITICAL AND MORAL SUBJECTS.

By MARY WOLLSTONECRAFT.

LONDON:

PRINTED FOR J. JOHNSON, N° 72, ST. PAUL'S CHURCH YARD.

1792.

A copy of the first edition of Wollstonecraft's classic feminist text belonging to her friend and disciple Mary Hays, whose signature appears on the title page.

to a wealthy widow. After a succession of low-paying jobs –
the only ones open to women at the time – she turned to
writing. In 1786 she wrote to her mentor, the radical publisher
Joseph Johnson, about her current "situation" as governess to
an Irish family: "A state of dependance must ever be irksome
to me . . . I have most of the [n]ative comforts of life – yet
when weighed with liberty they are of little value."* This
spirit of independence was the defining principle of her life. In
her struggle to achieve emotional and financial freedom, she
would repeatedly defy the conventions of the day; at a time
when few women did so, she traveled alone, first to Portugal to
attend a dying friend, then to revolutionary France, where
she lived openly with the American adventurer Gilbert Imlay,
whose child she bore. Finally, with their infant daughter, she
ventured to remote outposts in Scandinavia, where Imlay sent
her to unravel his business difficulties.

Abandoned and alone with her daughter after returning
to England, Wollstonecraft turned to her publisher, who supplied her with steady work as a translator, essayist, and review-
er, enabling her to regain emotional balance after she twice
attempted suicide. She rejoined the circle of artists and intellectuals that met regularly in Johnson's quarters, and there she
became reacquainted with William Godwin, whom she had
offended – by talking too much – during their first encounter
four years before. Perhaps it was fated that the two authors
should fall in love. It was unfortunate that their interlude of
happiness ended so abruptly with Wollstonecraft's death following childbirth. Although Godwin's frank and confessional
homage to her, *Memoirs of the Author of A Vindication of the
Rights of Woman* (1798), scandalized his contemporaries, future
generations would see the work for what it was: a loving
tribute to the woman whose life and work shaped the future
role of women in society.

you that when weakness claims indulg...
...t seems to justify the despotism of
strength. Indeed the preface, and even
pamphlet, is too full of yourself — In...
...ies ought to be made before they are
answered; and till a work strongly inter...
the public true modesty should keep...
author in the back ground — for it is o...
about the character and life of a good...
author that anxiety is active — ...
...is but a blossom.

       I am Madam
          yours &c

        Mary Wollstonecraft

Store Street Novr 25th, 92

St. Paul's Do you seemed uneasy when you w...
...ontrary to my first intention, I have put now
...en to Mr. J. who desires me to tell you that
...ry willingly waves the privilege seniority, then...

**Autograph letter (detail) from Mary
Wollstonecraft (November 25, 1792)
counseling Mary Hays to revise the
Preface to her Letters and Essays,
which, like the main text, "is too full
of yourself."**

The Mary Wollstonecraft material in the Pforzheimer
Collection consists mainly of correspondence, including letters
to her publisher Joseph Johnson, her friend and feminist disciple Mary Hays, and her girlhood companion Jane Arden.
Two literary manuscripts – a brief essay and a review – are also
found among the Collection's holdings, along with a portrait
in oils, a copy of the John Opie original (now in Britain's
National Portrait Gallery) commissioned by one of her
American admirers, Aaron Burr. Printed material includes first
editions of her writings, the most notable of which is a copy
of *A Vindication of the Rights of Woman* owned and annotated
by Mary Hays.

Mary Wollstonecraft Shelley (1797–1851)

In one of fortune's more ironic turnings, the most enduring
and popular work of the Romantic period was written not by
Shelley (or Byron or Keats or Wordsworth or Coleridge, for
that matter), but by an eighteen-year-old girl whose nightmare
vision evolved into the archetypal parable of modern civiliza-
tion – *Frankenstein*.

The novel had its genesis one stormy night by the shores
of Lake Geneva during the "wet, ungenial summer" of 1816,
when Lord Byron challenged each of the guests at his villa to
produce a ghost story. Stimulated by tales of the supernatural
and discussions about the origins of life that formed the
group's evening amusements, the future author of *Frankenstein*
heard in a waking dream those famous words which the
protagonist used to describe the unnatural birth of the creature
who has yet to lose his hold on the popular imagination:

FRANKENSTEIN;

OR,

THE MODERN PROMETHEUS.

IN THREE VOLUMES.

Did I request thee, Maker, from my clay
To mould me man? Did I solicit thee
From darkness to promote me?——
                    PARADISE LOST.

VOL. I.

London:

PRINTED FOR

LACKINGTON, HUGHES, HARDING, MAVOR, & JONES,
FINSBURY SQUARE.

1818.

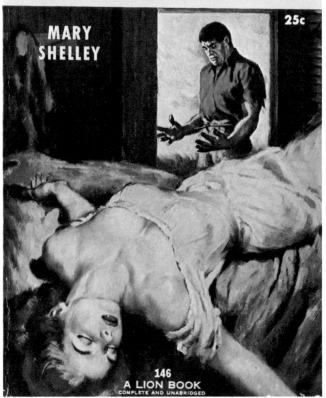

The first edition of *Frankenstein*
and a modern incarnation
(New York: Lion Books, 1953).

It was on a dreary night of November that I beheld the accomplishment of my toils. . . . It was already one in the morning; the rain pattered dismally against the panes, and my candle was nearly burnt out, when, by the glimmer of the half-extinguished light, I saw the dull yellow eye of the creature open; it breathed hard, and a convulsive motion agitated its limbs.

A year and a half later, when this remarkable first novel was published anonymously in an edition of 500 copies, the two most successful authors of the day, Lord Byron and Sir Walter Scott, had high praise for it. And when the story was adapted for the stage in 1823, it attained a popularity that it has never relinquished.

For a first-time novelist, Mary Godwin possessed imposing credentials. The offspring of a liaison between the anarchist philosopher William Godwin and the proto-feminist writer Mary Wollstonecraft, by the age of eleven she had already collaborated on a children's book, issued under the Godwins' Juvenile Library imprint. Raised on her late mother's principles and her father's theories, she put them into effect at the age of sixteen by running away with Godwin's disciple, a young unknown poet named Percy Bysshe Shelley. Despite the inconvenient presence of a pregnant wife and child, Shelley sensed that Mary Godwin could become the soul mate he had long sought, and he was willing to suffer for her sake the opprobrium which living out his "anti-matrimonial principles" would earn him. Soon after the suicide of his first wife, however, Shelley disavowed those same principles and, at the age of nineteen, Mary Godwin became Mary Shelley, partly to assuage family feelings and partly to legitimize their recently born son.

Frankenstein was not the only literary work Mary Shelley completed during the eight years she and Shelley spent together. She collaborated with her husband to write a travel book, *History of a Six Weeks' Tour . . .* (1817), and finished two mytho-

logical dramas and a second novel, *Mathilda*. She was at work
on a third, *Valperga*, when Shelley drowned off the Italian coast
in the summer of 1822. Like her mother before her, she faced
an uncertain future alone with her surviving child (three
others had died); also like her mother, she succeeded in making
a literary career for herself in spite of emotional devastation.
Following her return to England in 1823, she discovered that
she could not live on the meager annuity supplied by Shelley's
unsympathetic father and sought out opportunities to supple-
ment her income through a variety of literary pursuits: biographies, short stories, encyclopedia articles, book reviews,
and five more novels, the most famous being an apocalyptic
account of the destruction of mankind, *The Last Man* (1826).

In addition to her own writing, Mary Shelley served
posterity as her husband's editor, advocate, and interpreter.
Although Shelley's father tried to suppress all publications of
his son's work, she finally succeeded in overcoming his objec-
tions. In the Preface to *The Poetical Works of Percy Bysshe Shelley*
(1839), she defended her husband's political and philosophical
poetry, and in her extensive "notes" she anticipated later
critical efforts to place a writer's works within a biographical
context. She once wrote of *Frankenstein* that without her
husband's help "it would never have taken the form in which
it was presented to the world." Much the same could be said
of her own role as midwife to Shelley's creations. Over the
years her editions fulfilled the goal she had set for them: "to
lay the first stone of a monument . . . to Shelley's genius, his
sufferings, and his virtues."

• IN THE COLLECTION •

Over 400 items in Mary Shelley's hand make the Pforzheimer
Collection a major resource for the study of her life and
works. A wide variety of letters – more than a quarter of those
known to exist – document the course of her eventful life.
They begin with a series of notes written during her adoles-

First number of *The Liberal*, a
journal founded in Pisa by Byron,
Shelley, and Hunt. It folded after
only four issues.

cent flirtation with Shelley's best friend, Thomas Jefferson Hogg, and end with an announcement from her son to Leigh Hunt, informing him of her death. In between come exchanges with intimates from the early years (Byron, Peacock, the Hunts, Trelawny, Hogg, Jane Williams, Teresa Guiccioli, Isabel Baxter Booth); family (Shelley, Godwin, Claire Clairmont, William Godwin, Jr., her son, Percy Florence, and her daughter-in-law, Lady Jane Shelley); and later admirers, friends, and literary associates (John Howard Payne, Thomas Campbell, Cyrus Redding, Lady Morgan, Abraham Hayward, John Bowring, Dionysius Lardner). The collection also contains a sizeable body of letters to publishers (Charles Ollier, John Murray, Edward Moxon, Henry Colburn, and Richard Bentley), as well as copies of her published works, including the first editions of *Frankenstein* and two different editions of the exceedingly rare *Mounseer Nongtongpaw*, the amusing verse narrative to which she contributed as a child for her parents' Juvenile Library. Although the Collection's strength lies in correspondence, it also possesses literary manuscripts. These include poems ("O, Come to me in dreams, my Love" and "The Choice"), parts of a verse drama (*Proserpine*), and short stories ("The Dream," "The Sisters of Albano," and "The Trial of Love").

Leigh Hunt (1784–1859)

In 1821 Shelley and Byron invited Leigh Hunt to Italy, to join with them in founding *The Liberal*, a new journal that would serve as an outlet for their original compositions and for the writings of authors with a similar political and aesthetic point of view. Shelley's old friend Hunt was a natural choice. Poet, biographer, playwright, essayist, and critic – Hunt was all of these. But his fame rested principally on his accomplishments as an editor and crusading journalist. In 1808 he and his brother John began to publish *The Examiner*, a London weekly newspaper founded to promote "Reform in Parliament, liberality of opinion in general (especially freedom from superstition), and a fusion of literary taste into all subjects whatsoever." At a time when England was at war with Napoleon, such idealism had its consequences.

The Hunts' troubles began almost immediately. By 1810, when they reprinted an article against military flogging entitled "One thousand lashes," the brothers had already been charged twice with libel. Tried and acquitted a third time, the two nevertheless continued to voice their opposition to current government policies. In 1812, however, pointed criticism of the Prince Regent's profligacy and weakness led to a fourth trial for libel. This time they were convicted and sentenced to two-year prison terms. Hunt was confined in Surrey Gaol, where he kept on writing and editing articles for *The Examiner* as well as publishing his own poems and a political masque, *The Descent of Liberty*. Meanwhile, he became something of a jailhouse celebrity, receiving in his well-furnished prison quarters such notable figures as Byron, Hazlitt, Bentham, and Wordsworth.

Hunt's causes were poetical as well as political. In 1816, the year after his release from jail, it was Hunt who brought a young Shelley and a younger Keats together, just after having introduced their poetry to the public at large in the pages of the *Examiner*. Soon Shelley became not only a close friend but a benefactor, supplying the ever-increasing Hunt household with sums of money, large and small, and paying the expenses for the family's move to Italy. A week after Hunt's arrival, however, Shelley was dead. *The Liberal*, with Byron's lukewarm support, would survive for only four issues.

Hunt's literary career lasted nearly forty more years. He continued to write and edit essays, reviews, and commentary for leading journals of the day and to publish poetry and drama, although his writings grew less polemical in the years following passage of the Reform Bill of 1832 — so much so, indeed, that in

1847 Queen Victoria saw fit to award him a pension for his literary achievements. His partisan memoir in 1828, *Lord Byron and Some of His Contemporaries*, and his *Autobiography* in 1850 remain primary sources for the study of late Romanticism.

Among the Hunt items found in the Pforzheimer Collection are two bound volumes of *The Monthly Preceptor, or Juvenile Library* (1800), a small magazine that published submissions by schoolchildren. What is astonishing is not that Hunt's first published work, a prizewinning translation from Horace, appeared in its pages, but that the first efforts of both Thomas Love Peacock and Thomas De Quincey appeared there as well. Other markers of Hunt's subsequent long career are also in the Collection: first editions of his poetry, drama, and essays, along with original copies of the celebrated *Liberal* and some of the other periodicals with which he was associated. The Collection also has a number of his literary manuscripts: notebooks, drafts, proofs, and later copies of stories, essays, and poems, including his most anthologized lyric, "Jenny Kiss'd Me," a diverting essay on animal rights entitled "Angling," and the preface he wrote to the first edition of Shelley's *The Mask of Anarchy*. The correspondence, comprising almost 400 items, covers more than half a century. Besides letters to the Shelley circle (Byron, Trelawny, Hogg, and an important series to the Shelleys themselves), it includes family papers, exchanges with luminaries of the age (Jeremy Bentham, Walter Savage Landor, William Hazlitt, Thomas Carlyle), and correspondence with publishers (Charles Ollier, John Taylor, Henry Colburn, Richard Bentley, Edward Moxon), men of letters (Bryan Waller Proctor, John Hamilton Reynolds, Charles Cowden Clarke, William Bell Scott, Alaric Alexander Watts, William Tait, George Henry Lewes, Richard Hengist Horne, William Allingham, William Harrison Ainsworth), and actors (William Charles Macready).

NIGHTMARE ABBEY.

A ghastly figure, shrouded in white
drapery, with the semblance of a
bloody turban on its head, entered,
and stalked slowly up the apartment.

**Frontispiece for the 1837 edition of
Thomas Love Peacock's *Nightmare
Abbey* (Bentley's Standard Novels,
No. LVII), engraving by J. Cawse.**

Thomas Love Peacock (1785–1866)

Peacock began his literary career as a determined young poet. The letters he wrote as a child to his mother and grandparents often rhymed, and when he responded to a schoolboy essay contest – the topic was "Is history or biography the more improving study?" – his own entry, characteristically, was in verse. By the time he was thirty, however, he was coming to realize that his true métier lay in satirical fiction. Indeed, he could be said to have invented what is now called the novel of ideas, a category of fiction in which contemporary figures are caricatured and intellectual conversations predominate. His best-known work in this genre was *Nightmare Abbey*, a work designed, as he told Shelley, "to let in a little daylight on [the] atrabilarious complexion" of contemporary literary life. Although he used the machinery of gothic fiction as a backdrop, Peacock's real targets were the intellectual fashions and excesses of the age, especially the melancholic romanticism of Byron, the transcendental obscurity of Coleridge, and the reformist zeal of Shelley, each of whom appears thinly disguised among the novel's cast of characters.

The son of a London merchant, Peacock received a traditional classical education. His formal schooling ended before his thirteenth birthday, when he became a clerk in a commercial house, but he continued to pursue his Greek and Latin studies for the remainder of his long life. As a young man he also harbored literary ambitions, and had already published three volumes of poetry by the time he met Shelley in 1812. Although Peacock viewed the younger poet's eccentricity with amusement, the two became fast friends and intellectual companions. But while Shelley continued to develop as a poet, Peacock gradually became disillusioned with his own efforts in verse. In 1820, he wrote *The Four Ages of Poetry*, a mocking essay that inspired Shelley's impassioned rebuttal, *A Defence of Poetry*. Peacock argued that humanity would be better served if intellectuals directed their energies away from literature and toward commerce and the practical sciences. He himself had done precisely this. In 1816, having abandoned an epic poem he was working on, he turned the draft over to Shelley, who made it the basis for one of his own. And three years later, he accepted a position in the Examiner's Office of the East India Company, where he would remain for the next three and a half decades. As he ascended to positions of increasing responsibility, his literary output declined proportionately, but not before he wrote *Paper Money Lyrics*, a series of satirical poems in response to the financial panic of 1826, and a pair of novels in which he fixed his ironic gaze on the utilitarian ideology of his friend Jeremy Bentham and his colleagues at the East India Company, James and John Stuart Mill.

Although he never stopped writing poetry for amusement, in the 1830s a period of silence ensued, broken only by an occasional article or review. In the last decade of his life, however, Peacock again took up his pen, writing a final comic novel and summing up recollections of his friendship with Shelley in a restrained memoir, intended as an antidote to the florid biographies of the poet by other contemporaries.

· IN THE COLLECTION ·

The wide variety of Peacock manuscripts in the Pforzheimer Collection reflects the remarkable diversity of the author's interests and accomplishments, literary and extra-literary. The material ranges from a verse letter to the author's mother (written when he was seven years old) to the translation of an Italian play that would be his last published work. It includes such eclectic documents as "Ryotwar & Zemindarry Settlements," the examination essay he wrote to apply for a position at the East India Company; "The Science of Cookery," a collection of recipes and commentaries on food; and "The Present State of Steam Navigation," one of many papers generated by his interest in improving transportation links between England and India.

Literary manuscripts include notes and drafts for his novels *The Misfortunes of Elphin* and *Gryll Grange*; two different versions of his verse satire, *Paper Money Lyrics*; the unfinished Zoroastrian epic, "Ahrimanes," which Shelley subsequently turned into *The Revolt of Islam*; and a wide assortment of poems, essays, commentaries, and reviews. Although Peacock's correspondence is more limited in scope, the Collection holds a cluster of documents relating to his attempts to sort out Shelley's tangled legal and financial affairs as well as significant letters to his wife, Jane, and to Mary Shelley, Claire Clairmont, John Cam Hobhouse, and Thomas Jefferson Hogg. First editions of Peacock's printed works also occupy an important place in the Collection, including copies of two early books of poetry, *The Philosophy of Melancholy* and *The Genius of the Thames*, both with the author's own revisions, and one of two known copies of his first separately published book, *The Monks of St. Marks*.

Lord Byron (1788–1824)

Arguably the world's first superstar, Byron received both the adulation and notoriety that today would be fixed upon a rock musician or film actor. When the first two cantos of *Childe Harold's Pilgrimage* appeared in 1812, Byron's disaffected anti-hero captivated an English reading public wearied by almost two decades of war with Napoleon. The poem was an overnight sensation: as Byron later recalled: "I awoke one morning and found myself famous."

So famous, indeed, that the series of oriental romances which followed became instant bestsellers and the Byronic hero – brooding, dark, mysterious, erotically driven, but with a socially redeeming capacity for love – soon became a literary staple of popular culture. And the foremost Byronic hero was, of course, Byron himself. By deliberately cultivating a confusion between author and protagonist and by inserting himself as a character in his own works, he blurred the traditional distinction between autobiography and fiction. As a result, readers were quick to attribute to him the adventures of his protagonists and hungrily bought up successive editions of each new work. By encouraging such identification while at the same time disavowing it, Byron both anticipated the publicity-driven literary marketplace of a later age and suffered its consequences. He found, to his displeasure, that his private life was examined through the distorting lens of public opinion. Several well-publicized love affairs, the scandalous breakup of his brief marriage, persistent rumors of incest and homosexuality – all these topics were current in the drawing rooms and salons of Regency England, and in Byron's case the rumors were rendered even more sensational by the fact that so many of them were true. He became, as one of his more ardent female admirers put it, "mad, bad, and dangerous to know." Finding himself ostracized by polite society, he left England in 1816, never to return.

Exile, however, had compensations of its own. Freed from the hypocrisy and moral claustrophobia of England, he flourished in the more congenial climate of the Mediterranean, like others of his countrymen before and after him. His writing, too, broke free of the formal bonds that constrained the early satires and romances. During his years in Italy he experimented with a variety of literary forms, but it was in the ottava rima stanza that he discovered an instrument as supple and accommodating as the "countesses and cobblers' wives" he encountered in the palazzos and back alleys of Venice.

The salutary effects of exile on Byron's poetry became especially apparent in his masterpiece, *Don Juan*, written in installments between 1818 and 1824. In this open-ended satiric epic, Byron manipulated a poetic form elastic enough to cover the full range of human experience as he conceived it: adventure, romance, love, war, history, politics, metaphysics, religion, and, above all, the constancy of human folly. And in Juan, Byron created a more buoyant and essentially more sympathetic hero

A holograph draft of "Fare Thee Well" (March 18, 1816), the subtly manipulative poem that Byron addressed to his estranged wife.

than the melancholic Childe Harold, one whose amatory escapades (like those of the poet himself) continued to provide material for the London gossip mills.

Like his heroes, Byron was born for opposition. His sympathies lay with displaced workers in England, with an Irish populace crushed by British oppression, and, as he wrote in a note to *Childe Harold*, with "cudgeled and heterodox people" everywhere. From his early speeches in the House of Lords advocating Catholic emancipation and parliamentary reform to his sponsorship of *The Liberal*, the political and literary journal which he founded along with Shelley and Leigh Hunt, Byron consistently supported the struggle for human freedom. In exile, he first cast his lot with the outlawed Carbonari, whose vision of a united Italy would remain unrealized for two more generations. Afterwards, when Austria had crushed the Italian revolution-in-embryo, Byron turned to the cause of Greek independence, bankrolling and leading an expeditionary force against the occupying Turks. His death at Missolonghi in 1824 led to his apotheosis among the Greeks and among similar movements of self-determination from his day to ours.

· IN THE COLLECTION ·

Both the brooding poet who penned romantic lyrics and the cosmopolitan satirist who anatomized human folly are represented in the Pforzheimer Collection. The drafts of two important works epitomize the scope of Byron's genius: "Fare Thee Well," the strategically sentimental valediction to his estranged wife written shortly before he left England forever, and the last complete canto of the comic masterpiece *Don Juan*, finished only weeks before his fatal journey to Greece. Two other significant manuscripts in the Collection are the fair copies of the anonymously published jeu d'esprit, *Beppo*, the pivotal work in which he first found his comic voice, and of *Marino Faliero*, the first of his historical tragedies. Several minor literary manuscripts (including an extended verse letter to a boyhood friend, E. N. Long) also form part of the Byron holdings, along with fragments, translations, a portrait-in-miniature, and such documents as a letter of credit, a pharmacy bill, the codicil to his will, and a postmortem inventory of his effects taken by his friend Trelawny. The Collection also contains first and subsequent editions of most of Byron's published works, as well as his annotated copy of Ugo Foscolo's *Ultime Lettere di Jacopo Ortis.*

Byron has been celebrated as one of the wittiest and most articulate letter writers of all time. With over 150 pieces of his correspondence, the Collection offers a generous sampling of this remarkable epistolary talent. Beginning with notes from the easygoing years at Cambridge and terminating with a memorandum from the dark final months in Greece, the Pforzheimer's Byron holdings include important letters to Shelley, Trelawny, and Hunt, and to his wife Annabella, his half sister Augusta Leigh, and his last female attachment, Teresa Guiccioli. Among other correspondents are literary and publishing figures (John Murray, the Galignanis, Monk Lewis, Samuel Rogers, Lady Blessington, and Thomas Moore); celebrities of the day (Princess Caroline and John "Gentleman" Jackson, the boxing champion); old friends from England (E. N. Long, Francis Hodgson, Douglas Kinnaird, John Hanson, and R. C. Dallas); later associates from Italy (R. B. Hoppner, Captain Roberts, and Count Giuseppe Alborghetti); and political organizations (the Honorable Greek Committee in London, the Revolutionary Government at Naples).

In addition to Byron's own manuscripts, the Collection also maintains ancillary holdings of correspondence and other writings by his closest friend, John Cam Hobhouse, and by a number of the women who figured significantly in his life: his mother, Catherine Gordon Byron; his half sister and lover, Augusta Leigh; his estranged wife, Anne Isabella Milbanke; his only legitimate child, Ada Augusta; and several of his lovers, among them Caroline Lamb, Claire Clairmont, and Teresa Guiccioli.

Edward John Trelawny, crayon
and chalk drawing (ca. 1840) by
Seymour Kirkup.

Edward John Trelawny (1792–1881)

When Trelawny crossed paths with Shelley and Byron at the beginning of 1822, he appeared as a Byronic hero sprung to life. Mary Shelley described him as "a kind of half Arab Englishman ... six feet high – raven black hair which curls thickly & shortly like a Moors dark, grey-expressive eyes – overhanging brows upturned lips & a smile which expresses good nature & kindheartedness." She wrote in her journal that he had enchanted the Shelley circle with "strange stories of himself – horrific ones ... that harrow one up." Born the same year as Shelley, Trelawny had invented a character for himself, using fantasy to romanticize the events marking his unhappy childhood, unsuccessful naval career, and failed marriage.

It was Trelawny who encouraged Shelley to build his ill-fated boat in the spring of 1822, who broke the news of his drowning to his widow, and who superintended the pagan funeral rites on the beach at Via Reggio. The following year he joined the expeditionary force which Byron had raised in support of Greek independence. Leaving Byron on one of the Ionian Islands, he set out for the mainland, where he fell in with the heroically named warlord Odysseus, one of the rival claimants for power among the Greek partisans. Half a year later, when Byron died of a fever at Missolonghi, it was again Trelawny, arriving shortly after the poet's death, who took charge of the postmortem arrangements. Trelawny would remain in Greece for another four years, marrying the thirteen-year-old half sister of Odysseus, fathering two children, and surviving an attempted assassination in the mountain cave of his chieftain.

After Trelawny's wounds had finally healed, he settled in Florence and, aware that his finances were in disarray, set out to exploit his one marketable asset – himself. Channeling his creative energies into authorship, he commingled the events of his early life, his wayward course as a young midshipman, and his adventures (both real and imagined) into what became a best-seller, *The Adventures of a Younger Son*. First published in 1831, it soon went into another edition and was translated into French, German, and Swedish. This work, along with his friendship with Byron and Shelley, brought him a celebrity that would sustain him the rest of his life. With invitations to the drawing rooms of polite society, he settled into the permanent role of literary lion. In 1833 Trelawny embarked on a two-year tour of the United States, where further adventures included a Byronesque swim across the rapids below Niagara Falls to impress the famous actress Fanny Kemble. Back in England, he took up country living and married for a third time in the early 1840s. Further literary celebrity came with the publication of *Recollections of the Last Days of Byron and Shelley* in 1858, a book which he emended twenty years later in *Records of Shelley, Byron, and the Author*, a bitter redaction that reflected his increasingly critical attitude toward Byron and Mary Shelley. His fame endured into his old age, when he was cherished by the Victorian reading public as the survivor of a bygone era, hailed affectionately by Swinburne as "Last light left of our fathers' years." After death came in his eighty-ninth year, his ashes were buried, in accordance with his wishes, next to Shelley's in the Protestant Cemetery in Rome.

· IN THE COLLECTION ·

Among the Trelawny items in the Pforzheimer Collection are a manuscript, "The Death and Burning of Percy Bysshe Shelley," one of the many versions in which he mythologized his role as pagan priest at the poet's funeral; an account book from his continental travels that he kept in the period immediately preceding his friendship with Shelley and Byron; and a portrait of him drawn by his friend Seymour Kirkup, an expatriate artist and man of letters. The strength of the Collection's Trelawny holdings, however, lies in the letters – more than a hundred – that he wrote to Mary Shelley, Claire Clairmont, Edward Dawkins, Richard Bentley, the singer Adelaide Kemble (sister of Fanny), and Kirkup, among others. A series of more than twenty letters charts his relationship with Augusta White, the young woman who became his confidante in 1817 after his first marriage broke up. Despite her emigration to Canada and subsequent marriage to a prominent judge, the two continued to correspond for over half a century. Their final meeting, recorded in a diary now in the Collection, occurred in 1876.

Supporting Cast

Besides the circle of writers and poets already discussed, a large chorus of friends, relatives, spouses, and lovers, as well as rivals, critics, detractors, adulators, creditors, publishers, editors, scholars, forgers, and other literary camp followers, surrounded Shelley. These other lives are also documented in the Pforzheimer Collection. The following are some of the more important figures in this group.

Left to right:
Lady Mount Cashell
Edward Williams
Countess Teresa Guiccioli
(see List of Illustrations,
page 125, for full citations)

Diaries (1809, 1810) of the young
Shelley and Harriet Grove, his cousin
and first love. Most of Harriet's
entries concerning "dear Bysshe"
were canceled at a later date.

HARRIET GROVE (1791–1867) was Shelley's first cousin and first love, the object of an adolescent infatuation which, for a time, was reciprocal. Their courtship began in earnest in 1809 and was marked by visits, family trips, and a frequent exchange of letters. But what should have been a perfect match, a natural alliance of two prominent landowning families, soon went awry as Shelley's increasingly unorthodox opinions came to light. Although his schoolboy productions – an overheated gothic novel and a volume of adolescent poetry – raised some alarms, it was his correspondence that undid him. After Harriet showed some of the more opinionated letters to her mother, the informal engagement was quickly broken off. In a letter to his friend Thomas Jefferson Hogg, Shelley voiced his misery: "She is gone, she is lost to me forever she is married, married to a clod of earth, she will become as insensible herself, all those fine capabilities will moulder."* Harriet and the "clod of earth," a local clergyman's son, quickly produced four sons and four daughters. And Shelley himself soon found another Harriet to console him.

Harriet Grove's small, red, leatherbound diaries for 1809 and 1810 are now in the Pforzheimer Collection, as is a pocket diary with entries by Shelley himself from the same period.

HARRIET WESTBROOK SHELLEY (1795–1816) became Shelley's first wife when she was only sixteen. The daughter of a retired London tavernkeeper, Harriet had attended Miss Fenning's school at Clapham Common with Shelley's sisters and had made his acquaintance through them early in 1811. Singled out by school authorities for her association with the disreputable young man (Shelley had just been expelled from Oxford for his atheistic tract), she let herself be "rescued" by him, the rescue in this case taking the form of elopement and subsequent marriage. For the next three years, she dutifully followed Shelley's quixotic course as he moved from place to place and cause to cause. She bore him

To you my dear Sister I leave all my things as they more
properly belong to you than any one & you will preserve them
for Ianthe. God bless you both. My dearest [   ] Sister

When you read this I shall be no more an inhabi-
tant of this miserable world. do not regret the loss of one who could
never be anything but a source of vexation & misery to you all belonging to me. Be [   ] to except myself towards in the opinion of
everyone why should I drag on a miserable existence embittered
by past recollections and no one ray of hope to rest on for the
future. the remembrance of all your kindness which I have
so unworthily repaid has often made my heart ache. I know
that you will forgive me because it is not in your
nature to be unkind to any. dear amiable
woman that I had never left you oh! that I had always
taken your advice. I might have lived long and [   ] & happy
but alas I [   ] have ruined on my own destruction
I have no written to Bysshe. oh no what will it avail
my writes or my prayers would not be attended to by him
& yet I should see me this perhaps he might grant my
last request to let Ianthe remain with you always
dear lovely child, with you she will enjoy much happiness
with him none. My dear Bysshe let me conjure
you by the remembrance of our days of happiness to
grant my last wish do not take your innocent child
from Eliza who has been more than I have, who has
watched over her with such unceasing care. Do not refuse
my last request I never could refuse you & if you had
never left me I might have lived but now. Freely forgive
you & may you enjoy that happiness which you have deprived
me of.

a daughter in June 1813 and was pregnant again a year later when she found herself supplanted in her husband's affections by the sixteen-year-old daughter of Shelley's idol, William Godwin. Her life for the next two years remains something of a mystery, but one unambiguous fact emerges: death by suicide. On December 10, 1816, according to the London newspapers, the body of "Harriet Smith," described as a "respectable female far advanced in pregnancy," was taken from the Serpentine and carried to a receiving station of the Royal Humane Society. "Harriet Smith" was, in reality, Harriet Shelley. The long and distraught letter she left behind in her lodgings, jointly addressed to Shelley, her sister, and her parents, is now in the Pforzheimer Collection, along with some of her jewelry.

THOMAS JEFFERSON HOGG (1792–1862) was Shelley's best friend at Oxford and shared his enthusiasm for literature, his penchant for metaphysical speculation, and his love of the classics. Following their expulsion from the university for collaborating on a radical pamphlet, *The Necessity of Atheism*, Hogg settled down to study law. The friendship continued, however, surviving not only the efforts of their fathers to separate them but also Hogg's successive infatuations with Shelley's favorite sister and two wives. In 1813 Hogg published *Memoirs of Prince Alexy Haimatoff*, a pseudonymous novel, a work by and large free from the constraints of plot. In a review, Shelley hailed his friend's "bold and original mind" but, perhaps remembering the latter's perfidy, expressed dismay at the portrayal of "the loveless intercourse of brutal appetite." Hogg remained a fixture in Shelley's life until the poet left for Italy in 1818, when their relations cooled. Later, after Shelley's death, Hogg continued to display his odd proclivity for annexing his friend's female companions, eventually forming a common-law marriage with Jane Williams, to whom Shelley had addressed his last love poems. In old age, Hogg betrayed his friend one

Journal of C. Clairmont written in
the year 1814.

August. 1814

We took a walk in the Eg– and climbed
one of the highest of the hills– As we descended
a most violent storm of rain came on, and we were
wet through. The sky was entirely black and the
rain poured in torrents. One long strip of red
light alone marked where the sun had set.
S– said, "look there how the Sun in parting, has
bequeathed a lingering look to the Heavens, he
has left desolate." I thought this a most beautiful
thought. When we reached the valley it was
a very pretty sight to look on the lights from the
cottages reflected in a small clear stream that
flowed a bank beneath them. We went to bed
directly as our clothes must be dried in the night
They are the only ones we have got with us.

Monday 15ᵗʰ August. Rise at four. Misty
Morning and the wind bleak & cold. A peasant
takes us in his cart to Sugencourt, where we

Autograph revision of the journal
(August 14–22, 1814) kept by Claire
Clairmont when she ran away to
the Continent with Shelley and her
stepsister, Mary Godwin.

final time when he manufactured a self-serving biography that relied on doctored evidence to exculpate his own dubious behavior.

The Pforzheimer Collection's Hogg holdings include a school exercise book from Oxford; a heavily annotated copy of his travel book, *Two Hundred and Nine Days*; some seventy-five volumes, mostly classical, from his personal library; and over a hundred letters, including correspondence between Hogg and Shelley, Peacock, John Frank Newton, Jane Williams, Harriet Shelley, Elizabeth Shelley, Leigh Hunt, and Harriet Boinville.

CLAIRE CLAIRMONT (1798–1879) was Mary Shelley's trial, Byron's passing fancy, and Shelley's intermittent muse. The daughter of William Godwin's second wife, she was just three years old when she and her stepsister, Mary Godwin, were thrown together, and from that time on their fates were joined. When Shelley eloped with Mary in the summer of 1814, Claire accompanied them.

Like Mary, she kept a journal of their continental tour, and like Mary, too, she was determined to have a poet of her own. Two years later she succeeded, initiating an affair with Lord Byron, whose recent marital difficulties had just been sensationalized in the pages of London's newspapers. The affair with Byron was short-lived, but not short-lived enough to prevent her becoming the mother of his child. Though Byron quickly tired of Claire, refusing even to correspond with her, he reluctantly agreed to assume responsibility for their infant daughter, whom he eventually placed in a convent. An out-raged Claire had to be dissuaded from abducting the child, and her worst fears were realized when the five-year-old Allegra died of a fever in April 1822. The sad affair did have one positive result, however: it was through Claire Clairmont that Byron and Shelley became friends.

For eight long years Claire had been a dependent if not always welcome member of the Shelley household. Even before the death of Allegra, however, she had begun to plan for a separate and financially independent life. Shelley's sudden death in July of 1822 merely accelerated the process. From that time on, her life followed the pattern of so many single women in the nineteenth century: a series of positions as paid companion or governess. For the next twenty years, she moved back and forth across Europe, working for families in Russia, Germany, Italy, France, Austria, and England before she finally secured an inheritance from the Shelley estate in the 1840s. Thirty years later, a last glimpse of the woman whom Shelley had once likened to a "fiery comet" occurred in the pages of Henry James's *The Aspern Papers*, where she is portrayed as a faded spinster living out her final years in Italy. Reduced to taking in lodgers to make ends meet, she is pursued by a scheming bibliophile who hopes to pry away her last remaining asset – the letters a famous poet had written to her some fifty years before.

Parts of Claire Clairmont's journals can be found in the Pforzheimer Collection, including one for the summer of 1814 when she was the third party on Shelley's and Mary Godwin's elopement journey, and others from the winter and spring of 1818. The Collection also holds an insurance policy issued to her, fragmentary reminiscences of Byron, and about thirty letters, including several to Trelawny and one to Byron.

HORACE SMITH (1779–1849), equally successful as businessman and writer, inspired Shelley to observe: "Is it not odd, that the only true and generous person I ever knew, who had money to be generous with, should be a stockbroker! And he writes poetry too; he writes poetry . . . and yet knows how to make money, and does make it, and is still generous!" Appropriately, the anecdote was recorded by Leigh Hunt, who along with Shelley received timely sums of money from Smith. Smith had been one of Shelley's earliest admirers, and had already read with approval the almost unknown verses of the equally unknown poet when they first met at Hunt's cottage in 1816. At the time

Smith himself was one of the most successful writers in Britain. Four years earlier he had collaborated with his brother James on a collection of parodies entitled *Rejected Addresses*, a work so popular that by the end of the century it had gone through more than thirty editions.

After Shelley left England in 1818, Smith frequently acted on his behalf. He not only intervened in personal matters, but also served as an intermediary with tradesmen and publishers – in one case, having to placate agents from the Society for the Suppression of Vice who were outraged at the publication of *Oedipus Tyrannus*, one of Shelley's more outspoken political satires. Such trials never seemed to affect the friendship of the two men, and it was only his wife's illness that prevented Smith from joining Shelley in Italy. After amassing a fortune on the stock exchange, he retired at the age of forty-two to lead the life of a man of letters, producing fifteen novels as well as several volumes of essays, comic tales, and poems.

The Pforzheimer Collection numbers more than sixty-five items relating to Horace Smith, including a holograph poem, over sixty autograph letters, and one of his watercolors. About forty letters of his brother James are also in the Collection. Among the brothers' correspondents were such literary figures as Cyrus Redding, Robert Southey, Jane Porter, Bernard Barton, Thomas Hill, and John Wilson Croker; the painter Benjamin Robert Haydon; and the publishers Taylor and Hessey, John Murray, Henry Colburn, and Charles Ollier.

MARGARET KING MOORE, COUNTESS OF MOUNT CASHELL (1772–1835), described by Shelley as "everything that is amiable and wise," spent her adulthood living out the principles she had absorbed as a girl of fifteen from her governess, Mary Wollstonecraft. Bound to the Irish aristocracy by birth and marriage, she walked away from a joyless union at the age of thirty-three, leaving behind her titled husband and seven children, in order to live with George William Tighe, the man she genuinely loved. Changing her name to "Mrs. Mason," the fictional governess in Mary Wollstonecraft's *Original Stories from Real Life*, she settled with her companion in Italy, raised a second family, and, like her former mentor, authored several popular children's books as well as a treatise on child-rearing.

And as "Mrs. Mason" she repaid an emotional debt to her old governess, first by an exchange of supportive letters and occasional visits with the Godwin household, and then, in the spring of 1820, by opening her house in Pisa to Mary Wollstonecraft's daughter, by this time a mother herself as well as the wife of the poet Shelley. For a period of six months, the Shelleys and Claire Clairmont visited "Mrs. Mason's" villa on a daily basis, taking supper or tea, strolling in the carefully tended gardens, or studying in the well-stocked library. Shelley's allegorical poem, "The Sensitive Plant," has been interpreted by some as an act of homage to this friend whose "ruling grace" so inspired him.

The Pforzheimer Collection possesses a singular memento of this intergenerational friendship: a copy of Godwin's *Political Justice*, once part of Lady Mount Cashell's library, that both she and Shelley annotated. In addition, the Collection now holds the Cini archive, acquired from descendants of her second family in the late 1960s, and consisting of more than 130 items, including the manuscript of an unpublished novel, a private memoir written for her daughters, family letters, documents, and portraits, as well as inscribed editions and translations of her published works.

THOMAS MEDWIN (1788–1869) was Shelley's second cousin and schoolfellow, a retired half-pay lieutenant from the Indian Army, a prolific writer of indifferent poetry and prose, and the author of controversial biographies of Byron and Shelley. He was, however, a major catalyst in Shelley's life, introducing Trelawny and the Williamses into the expatriate circle in Pisa. Like other intimates of the two poets, Medwin managed repeatedly to trade off his reminiscences. Only six months after Byron's death, he rushed into print with his *Journal of the Conversations of Lord Byron: Noted During a Residence in Pisa, in the Years 1821 and 1822.* The sensational nature of his revelations ensured their instant bestsellerdom: the book was translated into French, German, and Italian and went through fifteen editions in sixteen years. After such success, it was perhaps inevitable that Medwin would turn his attention to his cousin. A brief epitome of Shelley's life had already appeared as an extended footnote to the *Conversations,* and in 1833 he expanded this into a series of articles in *The Athenaeum,* which were subsequently collected for separate publication. But perhaps it was money as much as anything else that drove him once again to become Shelley's Boswell. A series of unfortunate speculations in Italian art had dissipated most of Medwin's capital (the bulk of which had been supplied by his wife), and after unsuccessfully negotiating with Mary Shelley for his silence, he brought out the first full-scale life of Shelley in 1847. Although the trustworthiness of his recollections has traditionally been a matter of dispute, his writings remain the major source of information for certain periods of Byron's and Shelley's lives.

The Pforzheimer Collection contains almost forty of Medwin's letters and literary manuscripts, including correspondence with important publishers of the day such as Bentley, Colburn, Ollier, and Galignani.

EDWARD ELLERKER (1793–1822) and JANE CLEVELAND (1798–1884) WILLIAMS formed part of the congenial circle of expatriates who gathered around the Shelleys in Pisa in 1821. They had arrived at the urging of Shelley's cousin, Thomas Medwin, who had known Edward Williams as a fellow officer in India. Edward's common-law wife, Jane, was separated but not divorced from her rather unsavory sea captain husband. Edward, a writer and accomplished amateur artist, and Jane, a talented musician and singer, made an ideal complement to the more literary Shelleys, and the couples soon became quite close. The friendship was sealed after Shelley became a sailing partner of Williams, who as an adolescent had served as a midshipman in the Royal Navy. Soon the two families decided to share a house by the sea. Ten weeks later both men were dead – drowned on the return voyage from Leghorn, where they had sailed to welcome Leigh Hunt to Italy.

Jane Williams, the last in a series of Shelley's infatuations, figures prominently in some of his final writings – love poems which, the presence of their respective spouses notwithstanding, were openly addressed to her. Despite this, the two widows managed to remain friends, although the bonds created by their mutual tragedy were frayed in the late 1820s by Jane's indiscreet revelations concerning Shelley's estrangement from Mary before his death. Relations were further strained by Mary's growing dislike for Jane's new protector, Thomas Jefferson Hogg. Although they never married, Jane's liaison with Shelley's old college friend lasted until his death in the early 1860s.

The Pforzheimer Collection's holdings include twenty-five letters of Jane Williams, including a revealing one to Shelley written two days before he drowned, and sixteen to Claire Clairmont, most of which relate to the doomed marriage between Jane's daughter, Dina Williams, and Leigh Hunt's son, Henry. The Edward Williams material consists of his last letter to Jane, written from the quayside in Leghorn as he and Shelley waited for the weather to change; a fair-copy manuscript of his unpublished blank verse drama, *The Promise*, corrected and annotated by Shelley; a travel journal from 1819, illustrated with watercolors and pencil drawings; and a log from his naval days.

Countess Teresa Guiccioli Gamba-Ghiselli (?1800–1873), with whom Byron fell "damnably in love" in April of 1819, would be his last (female) attachment. For her he gave up a life of "miscellaneous harlotry" for one of "strictest adultery." Teresa Gamba-Ghiselli was convent bred, the second daughter among the fourteen children of a liberal but impoverished aristocrat from Ravenna. Like other young women of her class, she married to please her family, agreeing at the age of eighteen to become the wife of a wealthy count three times her age. Her affair with Byron changed her life, leading to a legal separation from her husband and further compromising the political status of her father and favorite younger brother, Pietro Gamba-Ghiselli, whose revolutionary sympathies would ultimately bring about their exile. It changed Byron's life as well; his connection with the Gamba family involved him in the Italian revolutionary cause – his first direct political engagement since his reformist parliamentary speeches eight years earlier. And when he subsequently went off to fight for Greek independence, he was accompanied by Pietro.

After Byron's death, Teresa Guiccioli preserved all the papers he had left behind and assembled a collection of portraits, relics, and books, by and about him. Most of the latter infuriated her, and out of a desire to provide a counterweight to biographers like Medwin, Hunt, Trelawny, Thomas Moore, and Lady Blessington, she began writing her own recollections, eventually publishing two hagiographical volumes entitled *Lord Byron jugé par les témoins de sa vie*. Although there were to be other men in her life after Byron, including the rich French marquis whom she eventually married, the memory of the five years she spent with her "amico amante in eterno" would dominate her imagination for the fifty years she outlived him.

The Pforzheimer Collection, along with the Biblioteca Classense in Ravenna, is now one of the two major repositories of the Guiccioli-Gamba Papers, an extensive archive that remained unknown for more than a century. At some point this archive was divided. Part of it, including almost 150 letters written by Byron to Teresa Guiccioli, emerged shortly after World War II and remained in Ravenna. The portion now in this Collection, however, surfaced only in the 1970s. Among its documents – long thought to have been destroyed – are letters to Teresa from Byron, Shelley, and Mary Shelley, as well as over 150 letters that she sent to Byron, many written while poet, mistress, and cuckolded husband were all uneasily coexisting in the same palazzo. Equally compelling are sequences of letters to Byron from "companions" like Marianna Segati, Margarita Cogni, and Arpalice Taruscelli, as well as revealing notes from several of the numerous and mostly anonymous women – "at least two hundred of one sort or another" – with whom he had enjoyed "vile assignations and adulterous beds" during his stay in Venice. Other parts of the Guiccioli-Gamba Papers include family documents and correspondence, autobiographical writings, commonplace books, early drafts of an unfinished account of Byron's life in Italy, as well as several heavily annotated books from her library, among them a novel by Ugo Foscolo with Byron's marginalia.

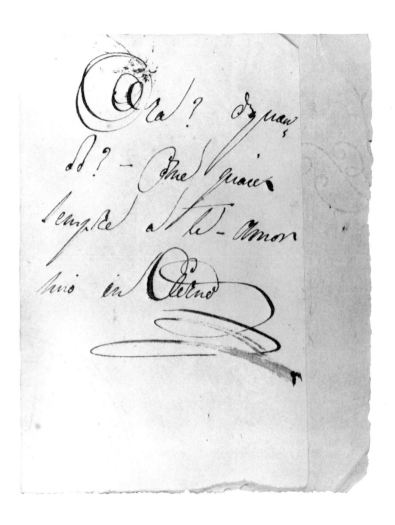

One of the many undated notes sent
in 1820 by Countess Teresa Guiccioli
to her lover, Lord Byron, while the
pair were conducting an affair under
the watchful eye of her complaisant
husband. In translation the text
reads: "Now? or when? – Ever as you
please – my Love to Eternity."

Detail from the bookplate of H. Buxton Forman, Shelley scholar, bibliophile, and forger.

Other Holdings

Besides the books and manuscripts of Shelley and His Circle, the Collection offers a wide range of collateral materials, among which are found early printings of other literary figures of the period; political and scientific treatises (including first editions of Thomas Malthus, Edmund Burke, Jeremy Bentham, Adam Smith, and John Stuart Mill); manuals on child-rearing, cooking, etiquette, and domestic economy; contemporary travel guides and road books; diaries and commonplace books; grammars and dictionaries; and almanacs and business directories. In addition, the Collection brings together topical pamphlets, broadsides, and other ephemera related to certain resonant issues of the day – for example, the Peterloo Massacre of 1819 and the 1820 adultery trial of the Queen of England. Finally, it selectively acquires critical, biographical, and textual studies related to the Shelley Circle, including archival material belonging to such nineteenth-century scholars as H. Buxton Forman, Thomas J. Wise, William Michael Rossetti, and Edward Dowden.

The Collection also has its share of curiosities. Among them are such Shelley relics as his baby rattle and infant shirt, pieces of jewelry which he gave to his first wife during their courtship, and a guitar he once owned. Other memorabilia illustrate the nineteenth century's fondness for physical remnants: a fragment of Shelley's skull, allegedly snatched from the drowned poet's funeral pyre by Trelawny; a lock of Mary Shelley's hair, sent to Hogg as a token of her affection; another lock of hair, belonging to Byron's illegitimate daughter Allegra, preserved in a volume once owned by his friend and fellow poet Thomas Moore; and an eyelash Leigh Hunt whimsically enclosed in a letter sent from Italy to his sister-in-law.

Materials that the Library of Congress would classify as "Literary forgeries and mystifications" have also made their way into the Collection, usually – but not always – by design. The popularity of both Shelley and Byron over the years has inspired successive generations of enterprising forgers to exploit a booming market for literary artifacts. The Pforzheimer Collection harbors a number of such items: forged manuscripts, fraudulent editions, and bogus association copies of books. Among them can be found samples of the work of Major George Gordon de Luna Byron, who passed himself off as the poet's illegitimate son, as well as a good number of the now infamous "certain pamphlets" which gained the bibliophile scholars T. J. Wise and H. Buxton Forman both fortune and disrepute.

The Pforzheimer Collection also maintains complementary holdings of books and manuscripts of literary personages from the eighteenth and nineteenth centuries, some closely related to Shelley, others more tangential. Figures well-represented include Robert Browning, Thomas Campbell, John Clare, Charles and Mary Cowden Clarke, William Cowper, John Wilson Croker, Walter Savage Landor, Thomas Moore, Samuel Rogers, and Robert Southey; in addition, limited holdings exist for other writers and artists, among them William Blake, Charlotte Brontë, Elizabeth Barrett Browning, Robert Burns, Samuel Taylor Coleridge, John Singleton Copley, George Crabbe, Thomas De Quincey, Benjamin Disraeli, George Eliot, William Gifford, Benjamin Robert Haydon, Washington Irving, John Keats, Charles Lamb, Sir Walter Scott, Sidney Smith, Thomas Noon Talfourd, William Thackeray, and William Wordsworth. Of this collateral material, a few items deserve special mention:

JOSEPH JOHNSON (1738–1809): a letterbook containing copies of the correspondence of this liberal bookseller, publisher, and in some instances, friend and benefactor to such leading intellectual figures as Thomas Paine, William Godwin, Mary Wollstonecraft, William Blake, William Cowper, Joseph

Priestley, Thomas Malthus, and Erasmus Darwin. The letter-book, which contains approximately 200 letters, both business and personal, spans the period from 1795 until his death.

WILLIAM BLAKE (1757–1827): the first edition of his earliest verse collection, *Poetical Sketches* (one of only fourteen known copies); *Songs of Innocence* (one of twenty extant copies), an early example of his distinctive illuminated printing process; and other works with his designs and engravings, including his *Illustrations of the Book of Job*, Edward Young's *Night Thoughts*, and Mary Wollstonecraft's *Original Stories from Real Life*.

JOHN CLARE (1793–1864): three bound volumes of his manuscripts, which include the transcript from which the first edition of *The Rural Muse* was set, as well as other poetry, prose, and correspondence; approximately seventy-five letters exchanged between his patrons and his publisher; and first editions of his works.

JOHN KEATS (1795–1821): first editions of each of the three volumes of poems issued in his lifetime, and two pieces of correspondence – one a short note to Fanny Brawne, the fiancée he never lived to marry, and the other, an engaging eight-page letter to his two brothers, covering literary, political, and personal topics.

ELIZABETH BARRETT BROWNING (1806–1861): manuscripts of two poems – a long, reflective piece entitled "The Dead Pan" and an abolitionist protest ballad, "The Runaway Slave at Pilgrim's Point"; first editions of her published works, including such rare juvenilia as an inscribed copy of her earliest book, *The Battle of Marathon*; and some twenty letters.

ROBERT BROWNING (1812–1889): more than 150 letters; the manuscript of his drama, *Colombe's Birthday*; proof sheets of later works like *La Saisiaz* and *Jocoseria* with the author's corrections; and first editions of his works, including such bibliographic rarities as his first published effort in verse, *Pauline*, and the separately issued parts (some inscribed) of *Bells and Pomegranates* in which such early experiments in dramatic monologue as "My Last Duchess" and "Pictor Ignotus" first appeared.

CHARLOTTE BRONTË (1816–1855): manuscript of *The Adventures of Ernest Alembert*, a fairy tale written at fourteen; and a half-dozen letters touching on both her writing and her personal life.

GEORGE ELIOT (1819–1880): five holograph notebooks (including one with extensive research for her novel *Daniel Deronda*), and one letter about her own struggles as an author: "If one is to have freedom to write out one's own varying unfolding self, & not be a machine always grinding out the same material or spinning the same sort of web, one cannot always write for the same public."

Because of its extensive Mary Wollstonecraft and Mary Shelley archives, works by other women of the period have always formed an important component of the Pforzheimer Collection. Particularly well-represented are a number of lesser-known women writers, especially Lady Blessington, Mary Hays, Felicia Hemans, Caroline Norton, Amelia Opie, and Jane Porter. The Collection also includes scattered holdings by such figures as Joanna Baillie, Charlotte Bury, Maria Edgeworth, Catherine Macaulay, Sydney Owenson (Lady Morgan), Mary ("Perdita") Robinson, Anna Seward (the Swan of Litchfield), Frances Trollope, and Helen Maria Williams.

III

Shelley: Life, Works, and Times

Shelley grew up in privileged circumstances. He was the son of a country gentleman and the grandson of a man who consolidated a fortune through shrewd practices and successive elopements with two young heiresses. Surrounded by an admiring mother and four affectionate sisters on the family estate in rural Sussex, he developed early on the need for female adulation and approval that would remain a constant throughout his life. This childhood idyll ended abruptly when, at ten, he was thrown into the rough-and-tumble world of an English public school, a formative experience that revealed those patterns of dominance and oppression against which he struggled in his later writing.

Both at home and at school, his precocity was evident. His scientific and literary experiments, iconoclastic philosophical speculations, and eccentric behavior all combined to gain for him a certain notoriety – at Eton he was known as "Mad Shelley." By the time he went to Oxford, at the age of eighteen, he had already published *Zastrozzi*, a lurid gothic novel, and had co-authored *Original Poetry* by "Victor and Cazire" with his sister Elizabeth. His father had been so impressed by these literary efforts that he instructed a local printing firm to indulge his son in his "printing freaks," a generous impulse he would soon have cause to regret.

Before his first term was over, Shelley had published his second sensational novel anonymously as "A Gentleman of the University of Oxford." Even more outrageous than its predecessor, *St. Irvyne* included set pieces on free love and identified its title character as an atheist. During this time he also published the pseudonymous *Posthumous Fragments of Margaret Nicholson*, purportedly written by the mad washerwoman who had

NOTE: Passages marked with an asterisk (*) are taken from original documents now in the Pforzheimer Collection.

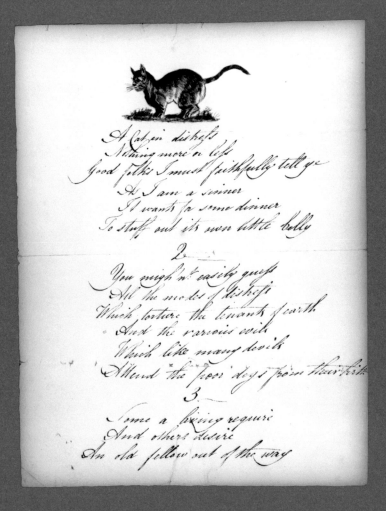

A Cat in distress
Nothing more or less
Good folks I must faithfully tell ye
As I am a sinner
It wants for some dinner
To stuff out its own little belly

2

You mightn't easily guess
All the modes of distress
Which torture the tenants of earth
And the various evils
Which like many devils
Attend the poor dogs from their birth

3

Some a living require
And others desire
An old fellow out of the way

Page 71: Percy Bysshe Shelley, plaster bust (1836) by Marianne Hunt, executed from memory fourteen years after the poet's death. Photograph courtesy of Sotheby's London.

Above: "A Cat in Distress" (?1803–?1805), presumed to be Shelley's first extant poem, copied by his sister, Elizabeth.

74

ZASTROZZI,

A ROMANCE.

BY

P. B. S.

——That their God
May prove their foe, and with repenting hand
Abolish his own works—This would surpass
Common revenge.

PARADISE LOST.

LONDON:

PRINTED FOR G. WILKIE AND J. ROBINSON,
57, PATERNOSTER ROW.

1810.

Shelley's first surviving published
work, begun when he was not yet
seventeen.

attempted to assassinate George III. He had also formed what would become a lasting friendship with a fellow student, Thomas Jefferson Hogg. According to a friend of Hogg's father, the two were distinguished by "a desire to be singular. . . . [They] gave up associating with any body else . . . never dined in College: dressed differently from all others, and did every thing in their power to shew singularity: As much as to say 'We are superior to everybody.'"* Their "singularity" also displayed itself in opinions so radical that Harriet Grove, the first cousin to whom Shelley was informally engaged, was pressured by her anxious parents into breaking off the relationship.

In March of 1811, Shelley and Hogg were expelled from University College, Oxford. The two of them had just written and published *The Necessity of Atheism*, a deliberately provocative pamphlet that the authors attempted to circulate by planting it in the shopwindow of an unsuspecting bookseller and by mailing copies to professors, heads of colleges, and bishops of the Church of England. After their expulsion, they went to London and began negotiating with their parents about their future. Hogg, able to effect a reconciliation with his family, was trundled off to study law in York. The more obstinate Shelley, however, remained unrepentant, staying on alone in London where he consoled himself with the company of Harriet Westbrook, a sixteen-year-old schoolmate of his sisters. From the Westbrook family parlor, with Harriet beside him reading Voltaire's *Dictionnaire philosophique*, he wrote to Hogg: ". . . marriage is hateful, detestable, – a kind of ineffable sickening disgust seizes my mind when I think of this most despotic most unrequired fetter which prejudice has forged to confine its energies. . . ."*

Despite these anti-matrimonial convictions, in little more than three months Shelley and Harriet eloped to Edinburgh, where they were married in an illegal ceremony. But he hadn't reckoned on the consequences. The daughter of a tavern-keeper, however well-to-do, would not have been regarded as a good match for the presumptive heir of a wealthy baronet, and Shelley's parents would undoubtedly have opposed the alliance had he bothered to consult them. When they learned that their son had "consulted [his] own taste in marriage," they exercised their one remaining option – cutting off his funds.

Meanwhile, the newlyweds were joined in Edinburgh by the ubiquitous Hogg. Later, when the three of them were living in York, Hogg attempted to put Shelley's free love theories into practice by trying to seduce his friend's young bride. Harriet's unwillingness to participate in the experiment precipitated an intense exchange of letters between the two friends, as Shelley attempted to explain and defend Harriet's right of refusal without sacrificing his allegiance to his principles. Before he resorted to argument, however, Shelley took the precaution of moving his household – which by now included not only Harriet but her elder sister, Eliza – to Wales.

In early February of 1812, Shelley, with his wife and sister-in-law in tow, set sail for Ireland. The next two years would be restless ones: Shelley and his entourage would migrate from Ireland to Wales to the West of England and back again to Wales and Ireland as he sought a viable means of putting his social and political agenda into practice. Among his baggage when he set out was the draft of a pamphlet in which he had "wilfully vulgarized the language . . . in order to reduce the remarks it contains to the taste and comprehension of the Irish Peasantry." Printed in Dublin ten days after his arrival, *An Address to the Irish People* was distributed personally by Shelley and Harriet, and by a hired servant who was instructed to thrust the tract into the hands of anyone who looked "likely." Although emphatically nonviolent (Shelley was mindful of the fate of earlier Irish nationalists), the *Address* staked out a decidedly anti-government position on two of the major issues of the day: Catholic emancipation and repeal of the recent Act of Union with England. Another work in this vein was the *Declaration of Rights*, printed in Dublin but circulated only after his return to England. This broadside, written under the influence of Robespierre, Godwin, and Thomas Paine, brought him under government surveillance when copies were discovered in a package opened by customs agents. The authorities at this time were particularly sensitive to such activities. Alarmed by the specter of revolution after an outbreak of Luddite violence and the recent assassination of a Prime Minister, government agents were closely monitoring Shelley's movements. In Devon his servant was jailed for posting copies on the walls of buildings. Later, the author himself was observed in a rowboat off the Bristol Channel, launching bottles and ingeniously contrived miniature boats into which had been fitted copies of the controversial tract. He was never charged with sedition, however, perhaps because he was both a minor and the son of a Member of Parliament. Besides writing and distributing pamphlets and attending political meetings, Shelley also attempted, in various locales, to form the nucleus of what might evolve into a utopian community. His most notable experiment involved the Tremadoc embankment project on the coast of Wales, a scheme to build a model town on land salvaged from the sea. Shelley signed on as a fundraiser, ironically at a time when he himself was about to be arrested for debt. A few months later, he left Wales abruptly, alleging that an attempt had been made on his life.

By the spring of 1813, Shelley had abandoned his efforts at organizational politics and returned to the environs of London, where he reestablished ties with Hogg and formed new friendships with William Godwin and Thomas Love Peacock, at that time a newly published poet. Through Godwin, Shelley met John Frank Newton and Harriet Boinville, liberal and sympathetic eccentrics who welcomed him into their circle. Newton was the author of *The Return to Nature*, a work advocating vegetable diet, nudism, and abstention from spiritous liquors. His sister-in-law, Harriet Collins de Boinville, the wife of a French revolutionary who had been aide-de-camp to Lafayette, still sported a wide red sash as a badge of republicanism and called herself *"une enfant de la Révolution."* For perhaps the first time in his life, Shelley found himself part of a group of congenial individuals who shared his views on religion, politics, sex, and diet. He moved first to Pimlico and then to Bracknell to be near Mrs. Boinville and her attractive eighteen-year-old daughter, Cornelia, who tutored him in Italian. Two years later, when the relationship with his wife had deteriorated, Shelley moved in with the Boinvilles, seeking refuge "from the dismaying solitude" of himself.

At this time Shelley also completed *Queen Mab*, the long poem he had been working on intermittently during the course of his travels. Published before his twenty-first birthday, his first major work was nothing if not ambitious. "The Past, the Present, and the Future," he modestly informed his publisher Thomas Hookham, "are the grand and comprehensive topics of this Poem." Its nine cantos, documenting a visionary journey through history, were augmented by a long series of radical prose notes that reflected Shelley's reading of Lucretius, Volney, Thomas Paine, Voltaire, William Godwin, and Baron d'Holbach. Turning away from direct action and pamphleteering, Shelley urged his publisher, if he did not "dread the arm of the law," to print 250 copies of *Queen Mab* on fine paper "to catch the aristocrats: they will not read it, but their sons and daughters may." It would be the sons and daughters of workers and not aristocrats, however, who would make the poem an underground bestseller. Its frequent piracies and reprintings guaranteed that Shelley's ideas would circulate among radicals of succeeding generations. The original edition, however, had only a limited circulation. Fear of prosecution led Shelley to excise his name from the title page and colophon and to remove the dedication to his wife Harriet from most of the seventy copies that he chose to distribute privately.

The same publisher declined another proposal from Shelley, who had assembled a collection of verses written during his adolescence. Hookham was, perhaps, alarmed by the poet's own assessment of this work:

> My poems will, I fear, little stand the criticism even of
> friendship. Some of the later ones have the merit of con-
> veying a meaning in every word, and these are all faithful
> pictures of my feelings at the time of writing them.
> But they are, in a great measure, abrupt and obscure –
> all breathing hatred to government and religion.

Among the poems from this collection preserved in what is now known as the Esdaile Notebook (now in the Pforzheimer Collection) are a pair of sonnets, "To a balloon laden with *Knowledge*" and "On launching some bottles filled with *Knowledge* into the Bristol Channel." Both poems describe the youthful Shelley's inventive efforts to find an audience; he would "publish" political manifestos by inserting them in fire balloons or empty bottles, trusting that winds or waves would convey these "vessels of heavenly medicine" to some landfall to bring "a ray of courage to the opprest & poor." Although some of the early verses in this notebook were eventually published in a more conventional fashion, the collection as a whole did not appear in print for another 150 years.

The disappointment Shelley felt over these publishing setbacks was compounded by a growing estrangement from his young wife Harriet. In 1812 Shelley had initiated a correspon-dence with William Godwin, whose heady theories of human perfectibility had made him the intellectual hero of reformers and revolutionaries in the 1790s. But when Shelley wrote him, praising *Political Justice* as an "inestimable book" that had "materially influenced his character," the anarchist philosopher could not have anticipated how "material" that influence would be. Beginning in 1813 Shelley became a frequent visitor in the Godwin household, taking on the roles of intellectual disciple and financial benefactor. At the same time, he found

How strange is human pride !
I tell thee that those living things,
To whom the fragile blade of grass,
That springeth in the morn
And perisheth ere noon,
Is an unbounded world ;
I tell thee that those viewless beings,
Whose mansion is the smallest particle
Of the impassive atmosphere,
Think, feel and live like man ;
That their affections and antipathies,
.... produce the laws
..... moral state ;
..... nutest throb
..... heir frame diffuses
..... st, faintest motion,
..... indispensable
..... stic laws,
..... on rolling orbs.

..... rsed. The Spirit,
..... ation, felt

QUEEN MAB;

A

PHILOSOPHICAL POEM:

WITH NOTES.

BY

PERCY BYSSHE SHELLEY.

ECRASEZ L'INFAME !
Correspondance de Voltaire.

Avia Pieridum peragro loca, nullius ante
Trita solo ; juvat integros accedere fonteis ;
Atque haurire : juratque novos decerpere flores.
* * * * * *
Unde prius nulli velarint tempora musæ.
Primum quod magnis doceo de rebus ; et arctis
Religionum animos nodis exsolvere pergo.
Lucret. lib. iv.

Δος πη ςῶ, καὶ κοσμον κινησω.
Archimedes.

LONDON:

PRINTED BY P. B. SHELLEY,
23, Chapel Street, Grosvenor Square.

1813.

All knowledge of the past revived; the events
   Of old and wondrous times,
Which dim tradition interruptedly
Teaches the credulous vulgar, were unfolded
   In just perspective to the view;
   Yet dim from their infinitude.
     The Spirit seemed to stand
High on an isolated pinnacle;
The flood of ages combating below,
The depth of the unbounded universe
     Above, and all around
Nature's unchanging harmony.

Printed but never published, the first edition of Shelley's radical poem *Queen
Mab* was withdrawn from circulation by the author. Fear of prosecution led
him to excise his name from the title page in most of the seventy copies that
he distributed privately; only a few escaped this prudent mutilation. Never
completely satisfied with the poem, Shelley continued to revise some of its
passages even after it was printed, as this copy of the first edition – once
owned by Jerome Kern – makes clear.

himself attracted to Godwin's daughter, Mary, the namesake of her famous mother, Mary Wollstonecraft, author of *A Vindication of the Rights of Woman*. Shelley courted Mary Godwin in the nearby churchyard of St. Pancras, where her late mother lay buried and where, on June 26, 1814, the two declared their love.

In *Political Justice* Godwin had written: "The institution of marriage is a system of fraud" – an avowal he would live to regret in the summer of 1814 when Shelley ran off to the Continent with his sixteen-year-old daughter. The veteran philosopher's rationalist principles were challenged by this impetuous act: not only had Shelley jettisoned a pregnant wife and child in favor of Mary, but the traveling party also included another of Godwin's wards, his young stepdaughter Claire Clairmont. Shelley, Mary, and Claire set a course through war ravaged France to republican Switzerland, following the itinerary of the hero of one of Godwin's novels. The journal Claire kept on the trip recorded their adventures and shows how much the three of them were intoxicated with her stepfather's melioristic philosophy:

> Shelley said there would come a time when no where on the Earth, would there be a dirty cottage to be found – Mary asked what time would elapse before that time would come – he said perhaps in a thousand years – We said perhaps it would never come, as it was so difficult to persuade the poor to be clean. But he said it must infallibly arrive, for Society was progressive and was evidently moving forwards towards perfectibility – and then he described the career made by man – I wish I could remember the whole – but half has slipped out of my memory – only I recollect men were first savages – then nomadic tribes wandering from place to place with their flocks – then they formed into villages – then to towns, and then improvement in mind, morals, comforts etc set in – and then next came Art – and then the Sciences – and from this point, Society would go on step by step to almost perfection.*

Contemporary engraving of St.
Pancras Churchyard, where Mary
Wollstonecraft was buried. In 1814
Shelley courted Mary Godwin here
beside her mother's grave.

After a journey down the Rhine, the trio returned to England and set up housekeeping in London. Shelley had neither seen nor written to Hogg since he had abandoned Harriet. Only in October did he inform his friend of his new domestic arrangements and of his "ardent passion" for Mary Godwin. "I do not think," Shelley wrote, "that there is an excellence at which human nature can arrive, that she does not indisputably possess, or of which her character does not afford manifest intimations." Hogg agreed. Letters exchanged among the three during the winter of 1815, now in the Pforzheimer Collection, document an open romantic attachment involving Shelley, Hogg, and Mary Godwin (and possibly Claire Clairmont), but whether their interrelations extended to sexual intimacy remains a vexed question. Certainly the daughter of William Godwin was more willing than the daughter of John Westbrook to entertain – at least in theory – the free love doctrines Shelley expressed in *Queen Mab*. The sixth month of pregnancy, however, was not a propitious time to inaugurate a *ménage à trois*. Reluctant to acquiesce, but unwilling to thwart, she could only temporize, writing to the importunate Hogg: "My affection for you although it is not now exactly as you would wish will I think dayly become more so . . . I ask but for time . . . time for that love to spring up which you deserve and will one day have." As a consolation, perhaps, she enclosed with the letter a lock of her hair. Shelley himself would not remain content with such half-measures. Two months after Mary had given birth prematurely – a fortnight later the child died – he was still advocating "participated pleasure," writing to Hogg to offer him a "share of our common treasure."

At this time, Shelley's finances were as tangled as his personal relationships. Even a poet cannot live on air, and Shelley, who derived no income from his writing and had no other employment, now had to maintain two households. In addition, he was temperamentally inclined to acts of generosity, many of them as spectacular as they were impractical. His financial situation, as a result, had always been precarious: ever since the rupture with his parents he had been hounded by bailiffs and, on more than one occasion, actually arrested for debt. He survived on the small allowance which his father had grudgingly reinstated; on credit, leaving a trail of unpaid bills behind him; and by reliance on a peculiar contemporary institution known as the post-obit loan, in which the heir to an entailed estate could borrow money against future expectations, usually at ruinous rates – three- or four-to-one was not untypical.

In 1815, when his grandfather died, Shelley's financial situation eased somewhat. His father, alarmed at the prospect that the family fortune would be jeopardized through his son's improvident post-obit borrowing, capitulated, agreeing to pay most of Shelley's debts and granting him an annuity of £1,000 a year. Financial problems would continue to plague Shelley for the rest of his life, partly because of the enormous sums he kept pumping into ventures like Godwin's failing bookshop. But after 1815 he was, in theory at least, independent.

Freed for the time being from financial constraints, Shelley was able to return to writing poetry. He began composing *Alastor* in late summer of 1815 after a restorative boat trip up the Thames with Mary Godwin, Peacock, and Claire Clairmont's brother, Charles. In the title poem, a young uncorrupted poet, one who seeks knowledge rather than love, is infected by the "spirit of solitude" (an Alastor), and searches for a visionary being who will embody everything "wonderful, wise, or beautiful." Shelley cautions against this sort of rootless idealism, but condemns as far worse the "morally dead" who live with no ideals at all. The following year he found a publisher for *Alastor*, which was issued in a slim volume with ten other poems including "The Daemon of the World," an indictment of social and religious tyranny distilled from the opening cantos of *Queen Mab*.

In the spring of 1816, Shelley, Mary, and Claire set out for the Continent a second time. The traveling party, which now

A compromising letter (January 7, 1815) from Mary Godwin to Shelley's best friend, Thomas Jefferson Hogg, with enclosed lock of her hair and inscribed packet (opposite). "Alexy" was her pet name for Hogg, taken from his novel, *Memoirs of Prince Alexy Haimatoff.*

included the four-month-old William Shelley, changed its
original destination from Italy to Switzerland after Claire
announced that she was pregnant with Byron's child, a product
of the recent liaison that she had initiated in London. The plot
to unite Claire with the object of her affection failed to produce the desired result: neither her absence nor her presence
made Byron's heart grow fonder. However, the clash of mind
with mind in the small circle that gathered at Byron's villa
above Lake Geneva that summer unleashed a storm of creative
energy that would permanently alter the topography of
English literature. Byron and Shelley both produced some of
their finest lyric poetry; Byron's private physician, Dr. John
William Polidori, began his tale, *The Vampyre*; and eighteen-
year-old Mary Godwin conceived *Frankenstein*, the most
enduring and popular work of them all. The summer was not
without its dark side, however. Byron's notoriety drew attention to the comings and goings between the famous poet's villa
and the cottage leased by the Shelley household; an enterprising local innkeeper even rented telescopes to curious tourists,
who were quick to impose their own interpretation on what

they saw. Soon rumors of a "league of incest" involving Byron, Shelley, and the presumed sisters spread to England. Shelley's ill-advised habit of signing "Atheist" after his name in hotel registers only served to confirm the public's worst suspicions.

That same summer Shelley and Byron began the literary and personal dialogue that would continue for the remainder of their lives. Together they sailed around Lake Geneva, reenacting a journey that Rousseau had made some sixty years earlier and visiting sites sacred to readers of *La nouvelle Heloïse*. In a long journal letter to Peacock, Shelley prefaced his day-by-day account of the excursion with a description of Byron:

> Lord Byron is an exceedingly interesting person, & as such, is it not to be regretted that he is a slave to the vilest & most vulgar prejudices, & as mad as the winds? I do not mean to say that he is a Christian, or that his ordinary conduct is devoid of prudence. But in the course of an intimacy of two months, & an observation the most minute I see reason to regret the union of great genius, & things which make genius useless. For a short time I shall see no more of Lord Byron, a circumstance I cannot avoid regretting as he has shewn me great kindness, & as I had some hope that an intercourse with me would operate to weaken those superstitions of rank & wealth & revenge & servility to opinion with which he, in common with other men, is so poisonously imbued.*

Though genius leveled many of the differences between them, the relationship would remain an unequal one: Byron, the most celebrated writer of his time, had no difficulty reaching the mass audience that Shelley sought but never found. Twelve thousand copies of the third canto of *Childe Harold* – which Byron was working on at this time – were printed by John Murray before the end of the year. By contrast, Shelley's most important poem from this period, his lines on Mont Blanc,

Autograph letter from Shelley to Lord Byron (November 20, 1816). The integral address leaf and wax seal are typical features of early nineteenth-century correspondence. Envelopes did not come into common usage until the late 1830s.

appeared only as a pendant to a small collaborative travel book he produced with Mary Godwin; when their *History of a Six Weeks' Tour* appeared in early 1817, fewer than 250 copies were issued and even fewer sold.

When Shelley, Mary Godwin, and Claire Clairmont returned from Switzerland in September of 1816, they temporarily settled in Bath so that Claire's pregnancy would not be detected by the Godwins and others. Concealing the true parentage of Claire's daughter Allegra would prove to be a continuing challenge to the embattled household, which had already been shaken by a series of crises. In October, Mary Godwin's half sister Fanny Imlay had committed suicide, and two months later Shelley's estranged wife, Harriet, drowned herself in the Serpentine. The tragic series of events was further compounded when Harriet's family sought to deny Shelley custody of their two children. Partly to strengthen his position in the impending custody battle, Shelley moved quickly to legalize his connection with Mary Godwin. He took this step in spite of his principled opposition to the institution of matrimony.

The wedding took place in London as the year 1816 drew to a close, much to the satisfaction of Godwin who, despite his egalitarian principles, was eager to see his daughter allied with the son of a baronet. Shelley's own feelings about the marriage are probably best expressed in the ironical tone struck in a letter to Claire written the day of the wedding: "The ceremony so magical in its effects was undergone this morning at St Mildred's Church in the city."* The nuptial rites did not impress the courts, however. In the legal proceedings which followed, the Lord Chancellor used Shelley's controversial writings to prove that he was unfit to be a father. As a consequence, when Shelley and Mary finally moved into their first permanent home in Marlow in March of 1817, it was with the knowledge that the children from his first marriage had been taken from him.

Compounding these personal misfortunes was a sense of apprehension brought on by the worsening political and economic conditions in England. Postwar depression and bad harvests had led to a state of unrest, and the government's sole response to growing demands for social justice had been to employ greater numbers of police spies and agents provocateurs. "The whole fabric of society presents a most threatening aspect," Shelley had written to Byron in the late fall of 1816. His own personal response to the crisis was to take up his pen, resuming his argument with the existing social order in two political tracts by "The Hermit of Marlow" and in the long, explicitly revolutionary poem, *Laon and Cythna*. The initial "Hermit of Marlow" production, *A Proposal for Putting Reform to the Vote Throughout the Kingdom*, was Shelley's first political tract since 1812. Hoping that his arguments for social change would forestall the revolutionary violence he feared, he had 500 pamphlets printed by his new publisher, Charles Ollier, and sought the widest possible circulation for them, sending copies to such radical figures as Robert Owen, Sir Francis Burdett, William Cobbett, and William Hone.

By spring of 1817 the political situation had deteriorated further. On March 4, Parliament voted to suspend Habeas Corpus and four weeks later passed a Seditious Meetings Act. And later that same year, when three labor leaders were hanged at almost exactly the same time that the royal heir apparent died in childbirth, "The Hermit of Marlow" was quick to point out the incongruity of the two concurrent events. The hastily issued pamphlet *An Address to the People on the Death of the Princess Charlotte* took ironic note of the reactions among his countrymen: the fate of the three working men was greeted with silence while thousands voiced their sorrow for the princess. Shelley's epigraph, "We pity the plumage but forget the dying bird" – taken from Thomas Paine's *Rights of Man* – reflected the radical message of the *Address*, the "dying bird" being, in this case, nothing less than the Spirit of British Liberty.

As the year 1817 drew to a close, Shelley grew more and more disillusioned with life in England. Beset by medical, financial, and legal problems, he found the prospect of living in the warmth of Italy increasingly alluring. And the imbroglio which accompanied the publication of his latest work, *Laon and Cythna*, could only have strengthened his resolve to quit the country. Inspired both by the current repression in England and by the still-fresh memory of the debacle in France, the controversial poem was nothing less than an attempt to rewrite recent European history, offering up the vision of a revolution unmarked by lust for power and revenge. This, in itself, was politically dangerous, but the love affair between Shelley's two protagonists, a brother and sister, was even more inflammatory. First his printer, then his publisher, and afterwards his friends objected to the incestuous relationship at the heart of *Laon and Cythna* and to the expression of religious opinions they believed would lead to prosecution for blasphemous libel. Shelley reluctantly agreed to some changes, and the poem was reissued in January of 1818 as *The Revolt of Islam* in a volume made up from the same printed sheets, but with a fresh title page and twenty-six cancel leaves.

Shelley left England for the third and last time in March of 1818. The traveling party included his wife and two children — the two-year-old William and six-month-old Clara — as well as Claire Clairmont, her year-old daughter Allegra, and two nursemaids. As they journeyed through France and across the Alps to Milan in a carriage and a calèche, Shelley again read aloud, not from the works of Godwin and Wollstonecraft as he had on the elopement trip, but from those of A. W. Schlegel. At first they hoped for a reenactment of the summer of 1816, this time on the shores of Lake Como. Byron, however, chose to keep his distance, determined to avoid the now-unwelcome attentions of Claire. Disappointed, the group resumed their wanderings, setting out on a restless itinerary that would take them through Leghorn, Bagni di Lucca, Venice, Naples, Rome, and Florence before they finally settled in Pisa two years later.

During this unsettled period, Shelley came to realize the price of exile. The friendships with Hogg, Peacock, and Leigh Hunt were attenuated now, kept alive only by infrequent letters from England. Chronic medical problems, growing estrangement from Mary, and the deaths of both Clara and William in less than a year added to his sense of isolation. A sustained note of dejection entered into his verse at this time, reflecting the poet's growing sense of personal alienation, which art could only partly redeem:

> Most wretched men
> Are cradled into poetry by wrong,
> They learn in suffering what they teach in song.

The lines are from "Julian and Maddalo," a poetic dialogue that grew out of an all-night conversation with Lord Byron during a visit to Venice in the summer of 1818. Shelley wanted "Julian and Maddalo" printed without his name because he felt the poem was too rooted in autobiography. He wrote to Leigh Hunt that he would recognize two of the characters and that the third, the figure of the Maniac, was "also in some degree a painting from nature." Most readers have identified Julian with Shelley, Maddalo with Byron, and the Maniac, whose tale of disappointed love is embedded in the poem, again with Shelley. Shelley meant to include "Julian and Maddalo" in a collection he described to his publisher as "all my saddest verses raked up into one heap." Other pieces intended for this volume were "Stanzas Written in Dejection – December 1818, Near Naples" and "Athanase, a Fragment." Athanase, like similar figures in *Alastor* and "Julian and Maddalo," is a solitary, an example of that hardy literary perennial, the isolated figure who is "too sensitive" for the world:

There was a Youth, who, as with toil & travel
Had grown quite weak & grey before his time;
Nor any could the restless griefs unravel

Which burned within him, withering up his prime
And goading him, like fiends, from land to land.*

These quasi-autobiographical pieces, all written in the same
pessimistic and introspective mode, would be published only
after Shelley's death. They were not the only works to emerge
from this unhappy period, however. He had begun his most
ambitious work, *Prometheus Unbound*, while staying in Byron's
villa at Este in the fall of 1818 and finished it in Florence, more
than a year later. But most of it was written, according to his
own account, in the open air, "upon the mountainous ruins of
the Baths of Caracalla ... under the bright blue sky of Rome."
In its Preface, Shelley acknowledged his "passion for reforming
the world," but defended his poetry from the charge of didacti-
cism, arguing that "until the mind can love, and admire, and
trust, and hope, and endure, reasoned principles of moral con-
duct are seeds cast upon the highway of life which the uncon-
scious passenger tramples into dust." In his lyric drama, a radical
reworking of Aeschylus, Shelley connects the transformation of
individual consciousness with the renewal of the social and
political order. The gifts that Shelley's modern Prometheus
offers the human race include a vision of a new earth, free from
the tyrannies of church and state, a world in which man remains

Sceptreless, free, uncircumscribed ...
Equal, unclassed, tribeless and nationless,
Exempt from awe, worship, degree – the King
Over himself. . . .

Prometheus Unbound, Shelley advised his publisher, "is my
favourite poem. I charge you, therefore, specially to pet him and

PROMETHEUS UNBOUND

A LYRICAL DRAMA

IN FOUR ACTS

WITH OTHER POEMS

BY

PERCY BYSSHE SHELLEY

AUDISNE HÆC, AMPHIARAE, SUB TERRAM ABDITE?

LONDON
C AND J OLLIER VERE STREET BOND STREET
1820

The modest phrase "with other poems," which appears on the title page, heralded the first appearance of some of the most enduring lyrics in English literature, including "Ode to the West Wind," "The Cloud," and "To a Skylark."

THE CENCI.

A TRAGEDY,

IN FIVE ACTS.

By PERCY B. SHELLEY.

ITALY.
PRINTED FOR C. AND J. OLLIER
VERE STREET, BOND STREET.
LONDON.
1819.

This tale of incest and parricide was
the only work of Shelley's to appear
in a second edition during his life.

feed him with fine ink and good paper." Shelley had a realistic sense of his own limited appeal, however. He felt that the poem was "written only for the elect" and predicted that it would not sell more than twenty copies. He was essentially correct: when the volume was published in August of 1820, it was denounced in the *Quarterly Review* as a "tissue of insufferable buffoonery." Few of his contemporaries imagined that *Prometheus Unbound* would attain the status of a masterpiece or that the incidental poems published with it – "The Cloud," "Ode to the West Wind," "Ode to Liberty," and "To a Skylark" – would find their place among the most enduring lyrics of English literature.

In contrast to *Prometheus*, Shelley's *Cenci* – his first work for the stage – was a deliberate attempt to court popular success. He began the play in Rome in the spring of 1819 and completed it during the summer at Leghorn, after the death of his three-year-old son. Shelley intended that the tragedy, based on a historical account of incest and parricide in a sixteenth-century noble Roman family, be performed at Covent Garden, and he hoped that Eliza O'Neill, the foremost actress of the time, would be cast in the starring role of Beatrice. The controversial subject matter of the play concerned him, but he persuaded himself that because the crimes portrayed were "historical," the play would not offend contemporary taste. Concerned that his reputation would prevent him from getting a fair hearing, he took elaborate steps to preserve his anonymity. As it turned out, the caution was wasted. The manager of Covent Garden, even without knowing the play to be Shelley's, found the work "so objectionable" that he refused to submit it to his leading actress. It would not be staged until 1886, when the Shelley Society sponsored a private performance by a group of professional actors. Even then *The Cenci* was denounced as a "moral outrage." The printed version fared better: it outsold all of Shelley's other works and was the only one to appear in an authorized second edition during his lifetime.

Shelley's own sense of "moral outrage," unlike that of easily scandalized contemporaries, was reserved for the social injustice endemic in post-Napoleonic Europe. "The torrent of my indignation had not yet done boiling in my veins,"* he wrote to his publisher in September of 1819, when news reached him

concerning an episode that radicalized the advocates of reform in England. On August 16 a party of mounted militia charged a peaceful assembly of 80,000 people who had gathered on a Sunday afternoon at St. Peter's Field in Manchester to protest parliamentary inequities. About a dozen died and scores were injured in what became known as the Peterloo Massacre. Shelley first heard of the incident through newspaper accounts supplied by Peacock, and responded almost immediately: "As I lay asleep in Italy / There came a voice from over the sea," begins *The Mask of Anarchy*. The voice induces an apocalyptic dream vision written in colloquial ballad stanzas, which Shelley characterized as a poem "of the exoteric species," meaning that it was written for popular consumption. He concludes the poem with a stirring appeal for resistance:

> Rise like lions after slumber
> In unvanquishable number –
> Shake your chains to earth like dew
> Which in sleep had fallen on you –
> Ye are many – they are few.

The completed poem was mailed back to England for publication in Leigh Hunt's *Examiner*. Hunt, however, whose writings had already cost him two years in prison, was wary of lines like those in which Shelley portrayed the current Foreign Secretary:

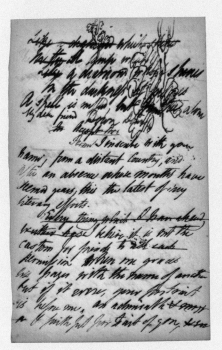
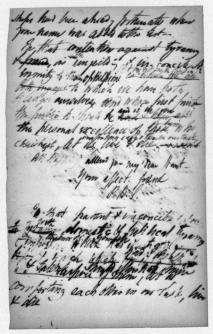

The first and last pages of a holograph draft of the "Dedication to the *Cenci*" which Shelley wrote for Leigh Hunt. Typically, Shelley worked on several compositions at the same time; these leaves, probably removed from a notebook, also contain a fragment of *Prometheus Unbound* (top left) and a stanza from *The Mask of Anarchy* (not visible).

Woodcut by George Cruikshank,
one of many cartoons published in
the wake of the Peterloo Massacre.

> I met Murder on the way –
> He had a mask like Castlereagh –
> Very smooth he looked, yet grim
> Seven bloodhounds followed him.
>
> ....
>
> He tossed them human hearts to chew
> Which from his wide cloak he drew.

Hunt's caution was not unwarranted – there would be no fewer than seventy-five prosecutions for seditious or blasphemous libel that year – and he shelved the poem until the passage of the Reform Bill in 1832 made its message seem less subversive.

Despite its caustic effigies of establishment figures and its appeal to class solidarity, *The Mask of Anarchy* is essentially a plea for moderation. Shelley argues that the symbiotic connection between tyranny and anarchy can be severed only by the conversion of oppressed peoples to nonviolence, thereby breaking the eternal cycle of "blood for blood – and wrong for wrong." Convinced that England was on the brink of civil war, he expressed his fears in a letter to Hunt:

> Some day we shall all return from Italy. I fear that in England things will be carried violently by the rulers, & that they will not have learned to yield in time to the spirit of the age. The great thing to do is to hold the balance between popular impatience & tyrannical obstinacy; to inculcate with fervour both the right of resistance, & the duty of forbearance.*

Shelley's own effort "to hold the balance" at this time prompted a return to prose. As political repression in England intensified, he described this shift in focus to a friend: "I have deserted the odorous gardens of literature to journey across the great sandy desert of Politics; not, you may imagine, without the hope of finding some enchanted paradise." Among the writings that date from this period was the unfinished draft of what he hoped would be "an instructive and readable book," *A Philosophical View of Reform*. Before breaking off in the third chapter, Shelley had already combined an ambitious historical survey of political change in the world with a close analysis of the current state of affairs in England. And unlike Plato, who banished poets from his ideal republic, Shelley viewed them as indispensable agents of social transformation:

> It is impossible to read the productions of our most cele-brated writers, whatever may be their system relating to thought or expression, without being startled by the electric life which there is in their words. They measure the circum ference or sound the depths of human nature with a com-prehensive and all-penetrating spirit at which they are themselves perhaps most sincerely astonished, for it [is] less their own spirit than the spirit of their age. They are the priests of an unapprehended inspiration, the mirrors of gigantic shadows which futurity casts upon the present; the words which express what they conceive not; the trumpet which sings to battle and feels not what it inspires; the influ-ence which is moved not but moved. Poets and philoso-phers are the unacknowledged legislators of the world.

A century would pass before Shelley's remarkable treatise, now in the Pforzheimer Collection, was finally published, just after the end of World War I.

In 1820, after almost two years of wandering, the Shelleys finally came to rest in Pisa, where they rented lodgings in a house overlooking the river Arno. The past year had been an eventful one for Shelley, encompassing stays in four different cities, the death of one child and the birth of another, the decline in his wife's mental health, and, in spite of all this, the completion of three major works and the genesis of several others. Meanwhile, in England, as the passions stirred up by the Peterloo Massacre began to subside, another political crisis caught the public's attention: the scandal created by the egregious behavior of the royal family.

Shelley followed the fortunes of Princess Caroline, estranged wife of the Prince Regent, in the pages of Hunt's *Examiner* and in *Galignani's Messenger*, an English paper published in Paris, to which many expatriates subscribed. After the death of George III in January 1820, his son, the dissolute George IV, who had been referred to as the Prince of W[h]ales, sued his wife (herself a rather robust woman) for divorce. George had married Caroline in 1795, but the ill-sorted pair had stayed together only long enough to produce Princess Charlotte in 1797. "Delicate Investigations" into the affairs of the Princess of Wales had occurred through the years: the Whigs always rallied to Caroline's side; the Tories traditionally took George's part. In 1814 Caroline had agreed to live abroad, but at the death of her father-in-law she determined to take her place as Queen. Her husband then instituted proceedings against her in the House of Lords. The grounds were adultery – potentially a capital offense when royalty was involved – and the correspondent was an Italian named Bergami, her former groom, on whom she had bestowed the title of Baron. The testimony against her was drawn mostly from the statements of government spies and suborned servants. The affair generated such an outpouring of popular support for the Queen that the regime itself was threatened. Hundreds of pamphlets and broadsides appeared, including Shelley's *Oedipus Tyrannus*, a two-act burlesque in which all the leading political figures of the day were satirized.

Years later, Mary Shelley gave the following account of the poem's genesis:

a friend [Lady Mount Cashell] came to visit us on the day when a fair was held in the square beneath our

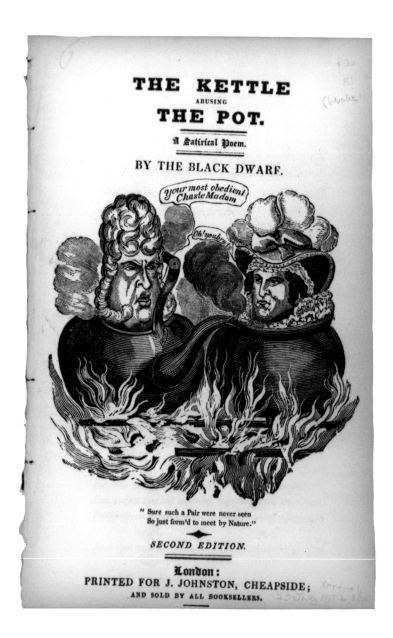

Caricature of King George IV and
Queen Caroline. His attempt to
divorce her, leading to an adultery
trial in the House of Lords, set off a
political pamphlet war.

windows: Shelley read to us his Ode to Liberty [probably the "Ode to Naples"] and was riotously accompanied by the grunting of a quantity of pigs brought for sale to the fair. He compared it to the "chorus of frogs" in the satiric drama of Aristophanes; and it being an hour of merriment, and one ludicrous association suggesting another, he imagined a political satirical drama on the circumstances of the day, to which the pigs would serve as a chorus – and [*Oedipus Tyrannus*] was begun.

Shelley sent the finished manuscript (a fragment of which now resides in the Pforzheimer Collection) back to his friend Horace Smith, asking him to arrange for its anonymous publication. The play, in which George IV assumed the title role, his Queen and ministers figured among the thinly disguised cast of characters, and the English people (Edmund Burke's "Swinish Multitude") appeared as the chorus, was duly printed as a pamphlet in December of 1820. The readily identifiable dramatis personæ, along with Shelley's exhortation to "Choose Reform or civil-war," all but guaranteed the swift suppression of the work. The authorities demanded that the entire edition be burnt: of the 200 copies printed, apparently only the seven that had already been sold escaped the flames.

At the same time that the Queen Caroline scandal was playing itself out, the first and only issue of an obscure London literary journal appeared, with a provocative essay by Shelley's friend Peacock, entitled "The Four Ages of Poetry." Having himself recently abandoned the life of a man of letters for that of a functionary in the East India Company, Peacock argued that literature had grown increasingly irrelevant to human improvement. Shelley's response, or "antidote" as he termed it, was *A Defence of Poetry*, written early in 1821, in which he asserted that Poetry (by which he meant Literature)

ŒDIPUS TYRANNUS;

OR,

SWELLFOOT the TYRANT.

A Tragedy.

IN TWO ACTS.

TRANSLATED FROM THE ORIGINAL DORIC.

—•—•—•—

——— Choose Reform or civil-war,
When thro' thy streets, instead of hare with dogs,
A CONSORT-QUEEN shall hunt a KING with hogs,
Riding on the IONIAN MINOTAUR.

—•—•—•—

LONDON:

PUBLISHED FOR THE AUTHOR,
BY J. JOHNSTON, 98, CHEAPSIDE, AND SOLD BY
ALL BOOKSELLERS.
———
1820.

This mock-heroic tragedy was among the hundreds of partisan tracts written
in response to the Royal scandal. Only seven copies of Shelley's barnyard satire
are known to have escaped the censors' flames.

reproduces the common universe of which we are por-
tions and percipients, and it purges from our inward sight
the film of familiarity which obscures from us the wonder
of our being. It compels us to feel that which we perceive,
and to imagine that which we know. It creates anew the
universe after it has been annihilated in our minds by the
recurrence of impressions blunted by reiteration.

Shelley intended to publish his answer to Peacock in the
second issue of *Ollier's Literary Miscellany*. When that magazine
failed, he had hopes that the essay would be issued as a separate
pamphlet. After his death, his widow prepared it for inclusion
in the *Liberal*, another doomed journal that also perished
before Shelley's rejoinder could appear. Unpublished and
unread, Shelley's *Defence* gained him no renown during his
lifetime. For later generations, however, the essay would eventually attain the same status as its sixteenth-century model,
Sir Philip Sidney's *Apologie for Poesie*.

   At the same time Shelley was in Pisa writing *A Defence
of Poetry*, his contemporary John Keats lay dying of tuberculosis
in Rome. Shelley had met Keats at Leigh Hunt's cottage in
December of 1816 and the two poets had maintained a guard-
ed but cordial relationship ever since, reading each other's
works with interest if not always with enthusiasm. When he
first heard about Keats's illness in July of 1820, Shelley urged
him to come live in Pisa. Keats, however, acting upon the
advice of physicians, went to Rome instead, accompanied
by a single companion who cared for him during his final
days. Though it was well known that Keats was consumptive,
Shelley had no trouble convincing himself that his fellow poet
had died "from the consequences of breaking a blood-vessel,
in paroxysms of despair at the contemptuous attack on his
book in the *Quarterly Review*." (A notion which Byron, with
characteristic lack of reverence, would call into question: "'Tis
strange the mind, that very fiery particle, / Should let itself

be snuffed out by an Article.") As a consequence, the poem which Shelley wrote in response, *Adonais*, can be read both as a traditional elegy and as another, more spirited, *Defence of Poetry*: "I have dipped my pen in consuming fire to chastise his destroyers," Shelley wrote of his lament for Keats, and then added, almost as an afterthought, "otherwise the poem is solemn & exalted." In a kind of Dantesque system of compensatory reckoning, the hostile (and parasitical) reviewers are reduced to "noteless blot[s] on a remembered name" while their victim, the wronged poet, is apotheosized as

> a portion of the loveliness
> Which once he made more lovely.

A small edition of *Adonais* was printed in Italy and shipped back to England for distribution, but Shelley's publisher at the time chose not to reprint it. As a consequence, the poem, which Shelley on at least three occasions had singled out as "the least imperfect of my compositions," would remain for a time one of the least read. The first English edition did not appear until 1829, seven years after Shelley's death, when an enthusiastic group of Cambridge undergraduates – Tennyson among them – arranged for its publication.

By the time *Adonais* was published in July of 1821, the Shelley household had been settled in Pisa for a year and a half. For the first time since they had left England, the Shelleys found themselves part of a community. They had been welcomed to Pisa at the beginning of 1820 by Lady Mount Cashell, now living under the alias "Mrs. Mason," who had known Mary Wollstonecraft and Godwin decades before. A few months later, they were joined by Shelley's cousin, Thomas Medwin, and at the beginning of 1821, by Edward and Jane Williams, an adventurous young couple whom Medwin had met in India. The cosmopolitan circle soon came to include Prince Mavrocordato, a leader of the nascent Greek independence movement, to

ADONAIS

AN ELEGY ON THE DEATH OF JOHN KEATS,
AUTHOR OF ENDYMION, HYPERION ETC.

BY

PERCY. B. SHELLEY

Αστήρ πρίν μὲν ἔλαμπες ἐνὶ ζώοισιν ἑῶος.
Νῦν δὲ θανὼν, λάμπεις ἕσπερος ἐν φθιμένοις.
PLATO.

PISA

WITH THE TYPES OF DIDOT
MDCCCXXI.

Adonais, which Shelley considered "the least imperfect of my compositions," was a moving elegy inspired by the death of his fellow poet John Keats.

whom Shelley dedicated his lyrical drama *Hellas*; John Taaffe, an Irish expatriate poetaster; Tommaso Sgricci, a famous *improvvisatore*, who specialized in the spontaneous composition of poetry; and Francesco Pacchiani, a professor of chemistry and metaphysics. It was also at this time that Shelley first met his "convent friend," Teresa Viviani, the nineteen-year-old daughter of the governor of Pisa, who would serve as inspiration for one of his most self-revelatory poems.

While Shelley was establishing himself in Pisa, his friend and rival poet Byron had also taken steps to regularize his life. In the spring of 1819 Byron had written to a friend: "I am in love – and tired of promiscuous concubinage – & now have an opportunity of settling for life. – " Before the end of the year he had followed the nineteen-year-old Countess Teresa Guiccioli, his "last attachment," from Venice to Ravenna, where he moved into the palazzo she still shared with her fifty-eight-year-old husband.

The dialogue between Shelley and Byron, begun on the shores of Lake Geneva in 1816, and resumed during their rides along the Venetian sands in 1818, was for almost three years confined to the letters the two poets exchanged. Then, in August of 1821, at Byron's suggestion, Shelley contrived "to take a run alone" to Ravenna, a visit which would have many consequences for both poets. A letter to Peacock contains an amusing description of Shelley's stay:

> Lord Byron gets up at two. I get up, quite contrary to my usual custom, but one must sleep or die, . . . at 12. After breakfast we sit talking till six. From six to eight we gallop through the pine forests which divide Ravenna from the sea; we then come home and dine, and sit up gossiping till six in the morning. . . . Lord B.'s establishment consists, besides servants, of ten horses, eight enormous dogs, three monkeys, five cats, an eagle, a crow, and a falcon; and all these, except the horses, walk about the house, which every

now and then resounds with their unarbitrated quarrels, as if they were the masters of it. . . .

(P. S.) After I have sealed my letter, I find that my enumeration of the animals in this Circean Palace was defective, and that in a material point. I have just met on the grand staircase five peacocks, two guinea hens, and an Egyptian crane. I wonder who all these animals were before they were changed into these shapes.*

During the summer days Shelley spent in Ravenna, his host read aloud to him the latest canto of *Don Juan*. The younger poet found the work "astonishingly fine," as he wrote to his wife, "something wholly new and relative to the age and yet surpassingly beautiful." He also noted, for Mary's approval, the recent changes in Byron's domestic arrangements: "LB. is greatly improved in every respect – in genius – in temper, in moral views, in health, in happiness. The connexion with la Guiccioli has been an inestimable benefit to him. . . . He has bad, mischievous passions, but these he seems to have subdued. . . ."*

Shelley perhaps might have been more concerned with his own "mischievous passions." While he was rhapsodizing over Byron's moral improvement, he himself was enmeshed in new difficulties: rumors of an illegitimate child he may have fathered in Naples were beginning to surface, and at the same time he had imprudently succumbed to another of his "infatuations," this time with the nineteen-year-old daughter of the governor of Pisa. When Shelley first met Teresa Viviani in November of 1820, she was in convent school, confined there by her father until such time as negotiations for an arranged marriage could be concluded. Naturally, Shelley found the situation irresistible and immediately set out to "liberate" her as he had so many other young women. He began petitioning on her behalf, but to no avail. The father remained obdurate, and the wedding plans went forward. Meanwhile, Shelley had placed her (with a change of first name) in a long, meditative poem on human love indiscreetly titled *Epipsychidion: Verses Addressed to the Noble and Unfortunate Lady Emilia V——, Now Imprisoned in the Convent of ——*. He later would describe the work as "an idealized history of my life and feelings." But perhaps it was not idealized enough: less than a year after its anonymous publication, Shelley himself arranged to have the poem suppressed. He must have realized that once he had been identified as the author, his allusions to the women in his life ("sun," "moon," "comet," and "planet") would be identifiable. Further, he must have been aware that his reputation in England was such that few readers would find the "platonic" intent in lines like the following:

> I never was attached to that great sect,
> Whose doctrine is, that each one should select
> Out of the crowd a mistress or a friend,
> And all the rest, though fair and wise, commend
> To cold oblivion, though it is in the code
> Of modern morals, and the beaten road
> Which those poor slaves with weary footsteps tread,
> Who travel to their home among the dead
> By the broad highway of the world, and so
> With one chained friend, perhaps a jealous foe,
> The dreariest and the longest journey go.

Despite Shelley's efforts on Teresa Viviani's behalf, the marriage took place in September of 1821, a fact he confided to Byron in a letter:

> My convent friend, after a great deal of tumult &c is at length married, & is watched by her brother in law with great assiduity. . . . They have made a great fuss at Pisa about my intimacy with this lady: pray do not mention anything of what I told you, as the whole truth is not known, & Mary might be very much annoyed at it.*

At the time of Shelley's visit to Ravenna, Countess Guiccioli's father and brother had just been banished for their part in the unsuccessful rising of the Carbonari against the political arrangements imposed by Metternich after the fall of Napoleon. Byron was determined to follow Teresa and her family into exile, but their destination was still in doubt because of his reluctance to return to Switzerland. Shelley also had misgivings about such a move. As he noted in a letter to his wife, Switzerland was "a place indeed little fitted for him: the gossip and the cabals of those anglicized coteries would torment him as they did before, & might exasperate him to a relapse of libertinism."* Shelley was ready with another suggestion – joining him in Pisa. The only alternative to a life of solitude, he wrote to Mary, "is to form for ourselves a society of our own class, as much as possible, in intellect or in feelings: & to connect ourselves with the interests of that society." Persuading Byron to settle in Pisa was a key step in forming such a community.

Shortly after Byron made his decision, Shelley wrote to Leigh Hunt in England:

> Since I last wrote to you I have been on a visit to Lord Byron at Ravenna. The result of this visit was a determination on his part to come & live at Pisa, & I have taken the finest palace on the Lung'Arno for him. But the material part of my visit consists in a message which he desired me to give you & which I think ought to add to your determination – for such a one I hope you have formed – of restoring your shattered health & spirits by a migration to these "regions mild of calm & serene air." –
>
> He proposes that you should come & go shares with him & me in a periodical work, to be conducted here, in which each of the contracting parties should publish all their original compositions, & share the profits. – *

Ravenna. July 14th 1820

In the year 1813 I first
read this book. I was
then in a state of great
agony of mind from a passion
which consumed me. — This
was in England. — — —
At present 1820 — I find
myself in similar circumstances
with the same book fallen
in my way — in Italy. —
It is an odd coincidence — "Coelum
"non animum mutant qui trans
"mare currunt." — most men
if I amail not having attained
the object of their desires—
have had oftener to deplore th
obtaining mine — f

On the eve of Countess Teresa Guiccioli's separation from her husband, her lover Lord Byron anatomized his feelings in the margins of this copy of *Ultime Lettere di Jacopo Ortis*, an epistolary novel by the Italian patriot and man of letters Ugo Foscolo.

AL LETTORE

Pubblicando queste lettere, io
tento di erigere un monumento
alla virtù sconosciuta, e di con-
secrare su le memorie del mio
solo amico quel pianto che ora
mi si vieta di spargere su la sua
sepoltura.

E tu, o Lettore, se uno non
sei di coloro che esigono dagli
altri quell'eroismo di cui non so-
no eglino stessi capaci, darai,
spero, la tua compassione al gio-
vine infelice dal quale potrai for-
se trarre esempio, e conforto.

Lorenzo A***.

I cannot love moderately, nor quiet
my heart with mere fruition. —
The letters of this Italian
Werther are very interesting—at
least I think so — for my innocent
feelings hardly render me a
competent judge. Byron

The periodical in question, *The Liberal*, did not come out until after Shelley's death. No major work of his ever appeared in its pages, although as editor Hunt included several lyrics and his translations from Goethe's *Faust*. Like Shelley, the journal had a short life: it folded after only four issues, and its English publisher, Hunt's brother John, was prosecuted. The incriminating text was Byron's irreverent travesty, *The Vision of Judgment*.

Byron moved his household to Pisa in November of 1821. Two months later, with the arrival of the expatriate adventurer Edward John Trelawny, what later became known as the Pisan Circle was complete. At this point, it might have seemed as if Shelley's desire for a community of like-minded individuals was fulfilled. Yet despite the apparent conviviality of his life in Pisa, with its riding and shooting parties, elaborate dinners, and male camaraderie, by the spring of 1822 Shelley was feeling increasingly dispirited. Thus, the summer move with the Williamses, from Pisa to Casa Magni, a converted boathouse on the sea near Lerici, came as a relief. But while the proximity of the attractive Jane Williams consoled him and inspired some of his finest lyrics, lingering anxieties over health, marriage, and the lack of an audience all contributed to a pervasive sense of failure and added a strain of pessimism to the ironically titled "The Triumph of Life," a work he did not live to complete.

A fragment of manuscript, layered with the scribblings, calculations, and notations typical of Shelley's working drafts, contains a discarded opening of this last major poem. Like *Queen Mab* and *The Mask of Anarchy*, it begins with a vision:

> before me fled
> The night; behind me rose the day; the Deep
> Was at my feet, and Heaven above my head
> When a strange trance over my fancy grew
> Which was not slumber, for the shade it spread
> Was so transparent that the scene came through
> As clear as when a vale of light is drawn
> O'er evening hills they glimmer. . . .
> And then a Vision on my brain was rolled. . . . *

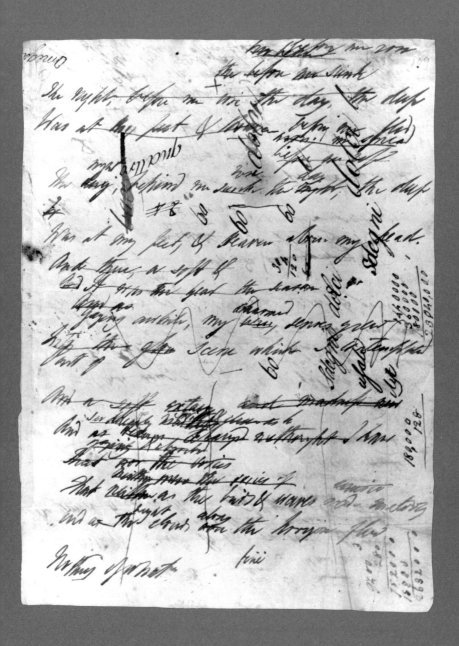

A fragment from the holograph manuscript of Shelley's last major poem, "The Triumph of Life," a work he did not live to complete. The layering and crosswriting are typical of Shelley's working drafts and show why editing his poetry presents such a challenge.

Central to this vision, realized in terza rima stanzas reminiscent of Dante and Petrarch, is the Roman custom of staging a triumphal procession after a military victory. In this case, the conqueror in his chariot is a personification of Life itself, and the captives, who follow in chains, include the world's leading historical figures: "the Wise, the great, the unforgotten." In the procession, hordes of youthful celebrants, "swift, fierce, and obscene," dance in front of the chariot, while behind follow "old men and women . . . with limbs decayed," but still persisting in the senseless dance. "Struck to the heart by this sad pageantry," the poet turns for guidance to the spirit of Rousseau, who, like Virgil in the *Divine Comedy*, interprets the spectacle. It is difficult to say how Shelley would have resolved the poem had he lived, but one thing is clear: its title notwithstanding, the work is no celebration of the *élan vital*; Life triumphs at the expense of humanity.

Shelley's withdrawal to Casa Magni in the spring of 1822 and the difficulties that he faced as he neared his thirtieth birthday did not interrupt the inquiry into political justice that he had begun when he was an undergraduate at Oxford. In a letter written only days before his death, he expressed his views to his friend Horace Smith in Paris:

> It seems to me that things have now arrived at such a crisis as requires every man plainly to utter his sentiments on the inefficacy of the existing religious no less than political systems for restraining & guiding mankind. . . . England appears to be in a desperate condition, Ireland still worse, & no class of those who subsist on the public labour will be persuaded that their claims on it must be diminished. But the government must content itself with less in taxes, the landholder must submit to receive less rent, & the fundholder a diminished interest, – or they will all get nothing, or something worse [than] nothing.*

Despite this dark reading of contemporary events, he had found a momentary stay against confusion on the shores of the Mediterranean:

> I still inhabit this divine bay, reading Spanish dramas &
> sailing & listening to the most enchanting music. We have
> some friends on a visit to us, & my only regret is that the
> summer must ever pass. . . .*

Other friends were also expected. In April of 1822, Shelley had requested his banker to "be so good as to pay to Mr Leigh Hunt . . . the amount of my quarter's income."* With the £220, Hunt was able to settle his affairs in England and to move with his wife and six children to Pisa, where the first floor of Byron's palazzo had been prepared for them. On July 1, Shelley sailed with Williams from Lerici to Leghorn to welcome the Hunts. Sadly, the reunion would be a brief one. On the return voyage seven days later, Shelley's small boat vanished in a storm off the Italian coast.

It was more than a week before the bodies of Shelley and Williams were recovered, washed ashore near Via Reggio. The corpses were much disfigured, and Shelley's body was identified by the books in his pockets, copies of Sophocles and Keats. It fell to Trelawny to break the news to the two widows and to negotiate the release of the remains. Italian quarantine laws at the time required that bodies of persons drowned at sea be buried where they were found. Shelley's body could be removed for burial elsewhere, as Mary Shelley desired, only if it was burned first. Trelawny, in the course of his long life, served up at least ten written versions of the dramatic cremation of Shelley on the beach at Via Reggio. In one account he described (with characteristic misspellings) Shelley's disinterment:

in the meanwhile Lord Byrons Carriage with Mr Leigh
Hunt arrived accompanied by a party of Dragoons and the
chief officers of the Town – In about an hour – and when
almost in despair – I was ~~however~~ paralized with the sharp
& thrilling noise – a spade made in comming in direct
contact with the skul. We now carefully removed the sand
– this grave was even nearer the sea and than the other –
~~not~~ and although not more than two feet deep ~~qu~~ a
quantity of the salt water has ozed in – this body having
been entered with lime 6 weeks previously we had
anticipated would have been almost destroyed — But
whether owing to the water or other cause ~~the~~ it had not
at all decomposed but was presisely in the same state as
when interred. – the dress & linen ~~had been~~ were black and
in shreds – and corruption had begun his work. . . . I was
now obliged to apply to ~~the~~ our guard to clear the ground
– as many boats from the Town filled with ~~people~~ partys
of well dressed people – particularly Women who seemed
particularly anxious to see so novel a ceremony their
curiosity being excited by the preparations to the utmost – *

On successive days, first Williams's body and then Shelley's
were exhumed and burnt in a pagan ritual with frankincense,
salt, oil, and wine thrown on the flames by friends in attendance.
Shelley's ashes were transferred to the Protestant cemetery in
Rome – where Keats is also buried – and eventually placed in
one of two tombs Trelawny ordered built in a niche of the old
Roman wall. The second he reserved for himself.

. . .

"Shelley, the writer of some infidel poetry, has been drowned;
now he knows whether there is a God or no." This notice in
The Courier was not untypical: clearly death did nothing to mute
the hostility that mere mention of the name Shelley provoked in
the mainstream English press. In the succeeding years, Shelley's

reputation changed: Satan became Ariel. *Queen Mab*, of course, always had a following of its own among working-class readers. The literary public, however, first came to Shelley through the 1824 edition of his *Posthumous Poems*, a collection assembled by his widow. Determined to keep his late son's name out of the limelight, Sir Timothy Shelley had the work suppressed, but not before copies had been circulated and favorably reviewed. At the same time he extracted from Mary Shelley, in return for a small annuity for herself and her child, the promise that she would not bring "dear S's name before the public again." Yet although he had bought the silence of his daughter-in-law, he could stop neither the pirated editions that continued to appear, nor the opportunistic memoirs in which his son's exploits – real and imaginary – were featured. Finally, in 1839, the aging Sir Timothy relented, grudgingly allowing his daughter-in-law to publish an authorized collected edition of his son's works. And while he continued to forbid a biography, he perhaps underestimated Mary Shelley's astuteness: her notes to the poems are as personal and intimate as the circumstances of her life and the growth of proto-Victorian prudery would allow.

The four-volume 1839 edition of the *Poetical Works* edited by Mary Shelley and the one-volume edition published a few months later solidified Shelley's reputation. But at least five unauthorized editions had appeared before them, and it was through these that he had already developed a following among young poets of the next generation, most notably Browning and Tennyson. As Shelley's fame grew, however, so did the temptation to repackage him, thereby separating the "lyrical" from the "political" Shelley in order to accommodate a socially conservative middle-class reading public. On the one hand, bowdlerized volumes like *The Beauties of Percy Bysshe Shelley . . . Free from all the Objectionable Passages* appealed to "respectable" readers. At the same time, literary pirates like William Benbow, a shoemaker turned publisher and militant radical, kept the poet's political legacy alive. Throughout the nineteenth century, successive generations of reformers would turn to his work: followers of Robert Owen and the Chartists in the 1830s and 1840s, Socialists and Communists in the later decades. The 1888 publication of *Shelley's Socialism*, a work co-authored by Karl Marx's daughter, Eleanor Marx Aveling, is but a single example. A few years later, George Bernard Shaw would bring the problematic nature of Shelley's literary reputation into sharp relief. He disparaged Shelley's highly touted "dexterity as a versifier" and denounced what he termed "bogus Shelleyism"–the etherealized image of the poet created by late-Victorian "literary *dilettanti*." Fired by Shelley's radical ideas, Shaw horrified a meeting of the Shelley Society by announcing that, like their idol, he was "a Socialist, an Atheist and a Vegetarian."

Like all great poets, Shelley has been the object of a continuing process of reappraisal and reinterpretation. Often despised, but never ignored, he has remained the same controversial poet who earned the hostility of contemporary reviewers and, later in the century, the disfavor of that high priest of mid-Victorianism, Matthew Arnold, who stigmatized him as "a beautiful and ineffectual angel, beating in the void his luminous wings in vain." In the twentieth century, the debate continued. Having found an eloquent advocate in another visionary poet, William

Butler Yeats, he was subsequently disparaged by other moderns like T. S. Eliot and Aldous Huxley. And after having survived both the benign neglect of the New Critics and the enthusiastic embrace of radicals in the 1930s and 1960s, he remains a voice to be reckoned with. More recently, both his poetry and critical theories have become a point of departure for structuralists, deconstructionists, new historicists, feminists, textual scholars, and other current literary practitioners. At the same time, his short but eventful life continues to be an object of fascination, even for those who choose to ignore the poetry. But it is the poetry that endures – the poetry and the forceful voice of a visionary "with a passion for reforming the world." More than 200 years after his birth, Shelley's insistence that poets are the "unacknowledged legislators" still serves as a rallying cry for those committed to the transformative power of the imagination and the "electric life" immanent in words.

Photograph (ca. 1900) of the Gulf of Spezia shoreline near Lerici. Shelley's last residence, "Casa Magni," is directly below this caption.

ILLUSTRATIONS

NOTE ON SOURCES

Passages marked with an asterisk (*) are taken from
original documents now in the Pforzheimer
Collection. Other quotations from Shelley's writings
are cited from *The Letters of Percy Bysshe Shelley*,
ed. Frederick L. Jones, 2 vols. (Oxford: Clarendon
Press, 1964) and from *Shelley's Poetry and Prose*, ed.
Donald H. Reiman and Sharon B. Powers (New York:
W. W. Norton & Co., Inc., 1977). Other quotations
from the journals and letters of Byron and Mary
Shelley are cited from *Byron's Letters and Journals*, ed.
Leslie A. Marchand, 12 vols. (London: John Murray,
1973–82); *The Journals of Mary Shelley, 1814–1844*, ed.
Paula R. Feldman and Diana Scott-Kilvert, 2 vols.
(Oxford: Clarendon Press, 1987); *The Letters of Mary
Wollstonecraft Shelley*, ed. Betty T. Bennett, 3 vols.
(Baltimore and London: Johns Hopkins University
Press, 1980–88).

This edition of 1,000 copies
was set in Bembo and Gill Sans and
printed by The Stinehour Press in
Lunenburg, Vermont, on acid-free,
archival paper. The book was
designed by Doug Clouse
at The New York Public Library.